School Leader Internship

School Leader Internship, 4th Edition, challenges school leader interns to build competencies in 52 leadership skill areas. This unique resource provides step-by-step guidance for interns, their supervisors, and their faculty on how to initiate an internship and evaluate interns' work. In this updated fourth edition, the content is organized around the latest National Policy Board for Educational Administration (NPBEA) Professional Standards for Educational Leaders (2015) and includes intern activities to develop skills in cross-content literacy, distributive leadership, equity in practice, professional learning communities, remediation strategies, school improvement planning, and special populations. This is a critical resource for leadership preparation programs nationwide and the thousands of school districts that support leadership candidates.

Special features include:

- *Beyond the Standards* provides further independent practice, reflection, and development for students in the areas of action research, ethical and critical reasoning, dispositions and interpersonal skills, new technologies, school partnerships, and social justice.
- *Self, Peer, and Superior Assessments* help students to plan according to individual need, experience, and goals.
- *Internship Plans* allow students to assess, analyze, and prepare draft internship plans.
- *Interview Suggestions* help students develop a network and gain insight into administrative and curricular responsibility.
- *Professional Development Activities* encourage students to analyze and evaluate their experiences and plan for the future.
- *Projects* allow students to synthesize their skills.

Gary E. Martin is Professor of Educational Leadership and Technology at Lamar University, USA.

Arnold B. Danzig is Professor of Educational Leadership and Policy Studies and Director of the Educational Leadership Doctoral Program at San José State University. He is also Professor Emeritus at Arizona State University, USA.

William F. Wright is Professor of Research, Foundations, and Educational Leadership at Northern Arizona University, USA.

Richard A. Flanary is an Independent Consultant and former Deputy Executive Director for Programs and Services of the National Association of Secondary School Principals (NASSP).

Margaret Terry Orr is Director of the Future School Leaders Academy at Bank Street College, USA.

School Leader Internship

Developing, Monitoring, and Evaluating Your Leadership Experience

4th Edition

Gary E. Martin, Arnold B. Danzig, William F. Wright,
Richard A. Flanary, and Margaret Terry Orr

Routledge
Taylor & Francis Group

NEW YORK AND LONDON

Fourth edition published 2017
by Routledge
711 Third Avenue, New York, NY 10017

and by Routledge
2 Park Square, Milton Park, Abingdon, Oxon, OX14 4RN

Routledge is an imprint of the Taylor & Francis Group, an informa business

© 2017 Taylor & Francis

The right of Gary E. Martin, Arnold B. Danzig, William F. Wright, Richard A. Flanary, and Margaret Terry Orr to be identified as authors of this work has been asserted by them in accordance with sections 77 and 78 of the Copyright, Designs and Patents Act 1988.

First edition published by Routledge 2003
Third edition published by Routledge 2012

Library of Congress Cataloging-in-Publication Data
A catalog record for this book has been requested

ISBN: 978-1-138-82400-3 (hbk)
ISBN: 978-1-138-82401-0 (pbk)
ISBN: 978-1-315-74173-4 (ebk)

Typeset in Palatino
by Apex CoVantage, LLC

◼ Contents

eResources ix
Foreword x
Preface xii
Acknowledgments xvi

Introducing School Leader Internship 1
Roles and Responsibilities 2
Assessing the Intern and Field Experiences 6
Outline of the Internship 7
The Developmental Nature of the Internship 8
Meeting Professional Standards 10

Stage One: Internship Assessment 13
1.1 Vita 13
1.2 Self-Assessment of NPBEA's Professional Standards for
     Educational Leaders 2015 13
1.3 Self, Peer, and Supervisor's Assessment of Dispositions 14
1.4 Other Assessments and Evaluations 16
1.5 District/School Assessment 16
1.6 Assessment Summary 17

Stage Two: Plan 19
2.1 Standards, Leadership Areas, and Activities 19
     Standard 1 Mission, Vision, and Core Values 21
        1. Vision/Mission 22
        2. Strategic Planning 23
        3. Data Collection and Analysis 24
        4. Effective Communication 25
        5. Negotiating/Consensus Building 26
        6. Collaborative Decision-Making 27

     Standard 2 Ethics and Professional Norms 28
        7. Ethics 29
        8. Local Norms and Expectations 30
        9. Philosophy of Leadership 31
       10. Interpersonal Relationships 32
       11. History and Traditions of the School and Community 33
       12. School Board Policy and Procedures/State and Federal Law 34

Standard 3 Equity and Cultural Responsiveness 35
13. Climate for Cultural Diversity 36
14. Cross-Content Literacy. 37
15. Equity in Practice 38

Standard 4 Curriculum, Instruction, and Assessment. 39
16. Analyzing the Curriculum. 40
17. School/Program Scheduling. 42
18. Learning/Motivation Theory 43
19. Learning Technology 44
20. Evaluation of Student Achievement/Testing and Measurements. 46

Standard 5 Community of Care and Support for Students. 47
21. Supervision of Co-Curricular Education. 48
22. Student Discipline. 49
23. Student Services 50
24. Special Populations. 51
25. Remediation Strategies. 53

Standard 6 Professional Capacity of School Personnel 54
26. Supervision of Instruction/Instructional Strategies 55
27. Staff Development/Adult Learning. 57
28. Personnel Procedures. 58
29. Faculty and Staff Evaluation 59

Standard 7 Professional Community for Teachers and Staff. 60
30. Issue and Conflict Resolution 61
31. Professional Learning Communities 62
32. Distributive Leadership 63

Standard 8 Meaningful Engagement of Families and Community 64
33. Community/Public Relations. 65
34. Parent Involvement 66
35. Community Resources. 67

Standard 9 Operations and Management 68
36. General Office Administration/Technology. 69
37. School Operations/Policies. 71
38. Facility and Maintenance Administration/Safety and Security 72
39. Student Transportation. 73
40. Food Services. 74
41. Supervision of the Budget 75

Standard 10 School Improvement. 76
42. Change Process 77
43. Current Issues Affecting Teaching and Learning. 78
44. Professional Affiliations and Resources. 79
45. School Improvement Planning 80

2.2 Skill and Performance Activities: Beyond the Standards 81
    46. Social Justice. 81
    47. Action Research. 88
    48. Dispositions and Interpersonal Skills 94
    49. New Technologies. 97
    50. School Partnerships 101
    51. Reflection in Action. 105
    52. Ethical and Critical Reasoning 110
2.3 Service Activities 122
2.4 Local Project Activity 123
2.5 Collaboration With the Site Supervisor 123
2.6 Internship/Leadership Experience Overall Plan Report. 124

Stage Three: Implementation 125
3.1 Interviewing. 125
3.2 Networking 126
3.3 Essential Competencies of Leadership: Theory Into Practice 126
3.4 Journal. 144
3.5 Log. 146
3.6 Organizing a Portfolio 146
3.7 Monitoring/Formative Evaluation. 146

Stage Four: Summative Evaluation/Final Report 149
4.1 Internship/Practicum Log 149
4.2 Professional Standards Assessment/Progress 149
4.3 Impact on Student Learning and/or Learning Environment. 150
4.4 Dispositions and Interpersonal Skill Assessment/Progress 150
4.5 Reflective Practice 150
4.6 Action Research/Project Leadership 151
4.7 Essential Competencies Development 151
4.8 Ethical and Critical Reasoning. 151
4.9 Social Justice. 152
4.10 New Technologies 152
4.11 Future Professional Development Plan 152
4.12 Developing the Portfolio 152
4.13 Vita Update. 153
4.14 Letter of Application 153
4.15 School Improvement Recommendations. 153

Appendices 155
Appendix A Sample Vita and Guidelines 155
Appendix B Sample Letter of Application and Guidelines 164
Appendix C National Policy Board for Educational Administration
                     Professional Standards for Educational Leaders 2015 168

Appendix D   National Association of Secondary School
              Principals 21st-Century Skills. 175
Appendix E   National Association of Elementary School
              Principals Standards 177
Appendix F   International Society for Technology in Education
              Standards for School Administrators 178
Appendix G   Sample Case 181

References 187
Index 197

■ eResources

Some of the tools in this book can be downloaded and printed for classroom use. There are also additional resources available that complement the material in the book. You can access these downloads by visiting the book product page on our website, www.routledge.com/9781138824010. Then click on the tab that says "eResources" and select the files. They will begin downloading to your computer.

eResource	Page
Dispositions Assessment	14
Sample Vita and Guidelines	155
Sample Letter of Application and Guidelines	164
Sample Case	181

Foreword

The authors of *School Leader Internship: Developing, Monitoring, and Evaluating Your Leadership Experience, 4th Edition*, have written a book that addresses the need of leadership programs to meet not only accreditation standards at the national and state levels, but also the real and practical needs of aspiring school leaders as they prepare for positions as school administrators. The internship is the *last safe place* to try out the professional duties, roles, and responsibilities that were presented in class as theories or were promoted at a conference as the next big thing to improve learning. Framing the internship experience around the knowledge, skills, and dispositions that encompass this book completes the training phase of preparation and begins the transition to a school leadership role. *School Leader Internship: Developing, Monitoring, and Evaluating Your Leadership Experience, 4th Edition*, presents information that the school leader needs to learn, consider, and perform in order to complete this transition.

Providing direction and a foundation for the book are the 2015 Professional Standards for Educational Leaders. These newly revised standards serve as the organizing framework for 45 skill and experience areas that challenge the aspiring school leader to effectively meet "challenges and opportunities of the job today and in the future as education, schools and society continue to transform" (NPBEA, 2015, p. 1).

The internship is the capstone experience for most leadership preparation programs and this book serves as a template for inquiry, reflection, and learning as the intern delves into the practical day-to-day issues of school leadership. The book weaves in self-assessments, projects, reflective practices, and a series of guided practice activities and performances that force the student to take a 360-degree perspective on school leadership. *School Leader Internship: Developing, Monitoring, and Evaluating Your Leadership Experience, 4th Edition*, breaks down aspects of school leadership and then guides the aspiring leader with the experiences that must be learned and internalized as knowledge and skill before moving on to a school leadership position.

The authors present knowledge of the applied world of school leadership that represents the training of future school administrators as scholar-practitioners. One must recognize school leadership in the 21st century as an inquiry-based professional position that requires school leaders to think, respond, and act in the best interests of children. *School Leader Internship: Developing, Monitoring, and Evaluating Your Leadership Experience, 4th Edition*, is a pragmatic scholar-practitioner overview of the world of schooling that helps move the training of school leadership to a level needed for 21st-century school success.

Jim Berry
Professor, Eastern Michigan University
Executive Director, National Council of Professors
of Educational Administration
2016 Chair, National Policy Board for Educational Administration

■ Preface

This text can be adapted to a variety of needs. It is written as a stand-alone text for a capstone internship. Depending on the nature of your institution's program, it may be used for a one-semester internship, field experiences used throughout a certification or master's program, or a combination of experiences in various required courses and the concluding internship. The text can also be used as supplemental material. You may require students to complete all or part of the text and/or provide the student with specific university requirements in a handout format to supplement and guide the use of the text.

The text may also be used for school district administrative training and development programs. Many districts are currently seeking new leaders from their faculties and sponsoring "grow your own" or local leadership development programs. The text moves beyond typical programs of giving out information on "how things are done in our district" to placing teacher leaders in positions of leadership and observing, coaching, and developing new prospective leaders.

Unique Aspects of the Text

Self, Peer, and Superior Assessments require the student to plan according to individual need, experience, and goals. This allows the intern to focus on specific strengths and areas needing improvement.

School/District Assessments require the student to plan according to school or district needs and goals. This allows the intern to serve the district as he/she works on increased learning, overall school improvement, and individual development.

Internship Plan requires the student to assess, analyze, prepare, and provide input into the draft internship plan for school and/or university approval. This allows the intern to take a leadership role in the development of the internship.

Projects require the intern to lead. This allows the intern to utilize all the leadership skill areas, as opposed to observation and/or carrying out assigned tasks. Many preparation programs require leadership of an action research project.

52 Skill and Experience Areas require the student to learn and perform leadership skills in a variety of essential school contexts. This provides the intern a wide breadth of experience.

12 Essential Competencies of Leadership: Theory into Practice requires the student to apply learning from previous coursework. This allows the intern the opportunity to reflect and form effective habits and increase learning from the field of educational research. This section is provided for review and focus, not to supplant previous instruction and study.

Interviews require the student to gather additional information and an overall perspective from leaders in various positions in the school or district. This helps the intern develop a network and gain insights and additional activities in various administrative/curricular areas. Interviews are recommended at the beginning of the internship.

Reflective Practice requires the student to learn the art of reflection. This allows the intern to develop the necessary skill of reflection in and on practice. It is highly recommended to stress the importance of this skill and to review reflections periodically.

Ethical and Critical Reasoning and Social Justice require the student to look deeper into leadership and the impact on diverse learners.

Future Professional Development requires the student to analyze and evaluate his or her experience and plan for further development.

Vita and Letter of Application require the student to develop a professional "accomplishments oriented" vita and relevant letter of application. This also assists the intern in gathering needed documentation for future leadership positions.

Final Report requires the student to analyze, evaluate, develop, and present a concluding professional report. This gives the intern the opportunity to take a leadership role in the evaluation of the internship and demonstrate the knowledge and skill gained from the experience.

Enhancements in the 4th Edition

This edition was revised to meet the newly adopted National Policy Board for Educational Administration (NPBEA) Professional Standards for Educational Leaders 2015. These policy standards serve as the framework for the Educational Leadership Constituent Council/National Educational Leadership Preparation (ELCC/NELP) standards for university preparation programs. In order to effectively meet the new standards, the text includes intern activities in the following new skill and performance areas:

- Cross-Content Literacy
- Distributive Leadership
- Equity in Practice
- Professional Learning Communities
- Remediation Strategies
- School Improvement Planning
- Special Populations

The 4th edition also includes a totally new section of intern activities termed *Beyond the Standards.* This section (2.2) lists and describes activities that move beyond specific NPBEA outcomes and require further independent practice, reflection, and development. These new skill and performance areas include:

♦ Action Research
♦ Ethical and Critical Reasoning
♦ Dispositions and Interpersonal Skill
♦ New Technologies
♦ School Partnerships
♦ Social Justice

Outline of the Text

The text is organized according to the four stages of an internship – assessment, planning, implementation, and evaluation. Stage One covers the necessary personal and district/school assessments. These include:

♦ Vita development and assessment
♦ NPBEA Professional Standards for Educational Leaders 2015 assessment
♦ Dispositions assessment
♦ District/school assessment and/or improvement plans
♦ Any additional personal assessments

This background information serves to assist the intern and school mentor in the following planning stage.

Stage Two covers the development of the plan. A variety of skill and performance areas are listed under each of the ten NPBEA Professional Standards. These areas comprise relevant skills and contexts that prospective school leaders need to experience in order to progress toward mastery of the standard. Suggested intern activities are listed under each skill and performance area. The intern must plan activities in each of the 52 areas. He or she is NOT required to undertake all of the suggested activities listed. The intern can choose from these activities or may design other activities related to the area. In this fashion, the internship plan can be individualized, while ensuring a sufficient broad base of experience and high level of expectation. This stage allows for consensus of the plan by the intern and school and university supervisors.

Stage Three covers the implementation of the plan. This section addresses interviewing a variety of school leaders to gain insight into differing organizational departments/areas and acquiring additional relevant intern activities. This stage also requires the intern, while implementing planned activities, to focus on observing theory in practice and reflecting in and on practice. This stage also describes keeping a log and journal and conducting formative evaluation. This stage assists the intern in completing all requirements for the final intern evaluation stage.

Stage Four addresses the final internship report. Although universities may require additional or differing final artifacts, the authors suggest completion and presentation of the following:

- Internship/Practicum Log and Portfolio
- Professional Standards Assessment/Progress
- Impact on Student Learning and/or Learning Environment
- Dispositions and Interpersonal Skills Assessment/Progress
- Reflective Practice Outcomes
- Action Research/Project Leadership Results
- Development in Essential Skills, Ethical and Critical Reasoning, Social Justice, and New Technologies
- Future Professional Development Plan
- Vita and Letter of Application
- School Improvement Recommendations

The authors believe that requiring a professional report with the breadth and depth of the above will inspire a more rigorous and meaningful internship experience.

Acknowledgments

Special thanks to the following authors and contributors:

To Ibrahima Poda, Dwayne Harapnuik, and Tilisa Thibodeaux, Lamar University, for writing section #49 New Technologies and intern activities for #19 Learning Technology and #36 General Office Administration/Technology.

To Karen Sanzo, Old Dominion University, for writing section #50 School Partnerships.

To Donna S. Azodi, Daryl Ann Borel, Cynthia D. Cummings, and Rebecca K. Frels, Lamar University, for writing section #47 Action Research.

To Jim Berry, Eastern Michigan University, for graciously writing the Foreword.

To Thomas Ross Hughes of Northern Arizona University, Cynthia McDaniels of Southern Connecticut State University, Theodore Gilkey of Salisbury University, Robert Scheidet of Stony Brook University, Janet A. Boberg of Northern Arizona State University, and Zachary Y. Mngo of Andrews University, for their helpful reviews.

And finally, to all the interns and school and university supervisors for their use of the text, dedication, and service to our nation's schools.

■ Introducing School Leader Internship

School Leader Internship: Developing, Monitoring, and Evaluating Your Leadership Experience is written to meet the specific national standards of NPBEA's Professional Standards for Educational Leaders 2015, correlated state standards, and individual professional goals. The intent is to assist aspiring educational leaders in the assessment, design, implementation, and evaluation of a university or district intern leadership experience. The term *leadership experience* is appropriate and signifies a radical departure from the traditional internship and/or district training program. In using a leadership development approach, the intern assumes the leadership role. In effect, it becomes a self-strategic plan requiring assessments, timelines, allocation of resources, benchmarks, ongoing monitoring and adjusting, evaluation, and reporting.

The internship is both a capstone of educational endeavor and a beginning experience in meeting the demands of a new position and new role in educational leadership. It is assumed that prerequisite knowledge, skill, and disposition are at an adequate level for entry into the new leadership experience. The internship requires a high level of knowledge, skill, appropriate disposition, and effort. The experience of leadership is the goal. The intern must assume responsibility and take the initiative to create meaningful experiences that build capacity in order to be effective in the internship.

Warren Bennis (1989) echoed this sentiment by stating

What is true for leaders is, for better or for worse, true for each of us: we are our own raw material. Only when we know what we're made of and what we want to make of it can we begin our lives – and we must do it despite an unwitting conspiracy of people and events against us. (p. 56)

The intern becomes accountable for the breadth, depth, and rigor of the experience. True leaders welcome this responsibility and the resulting balance of authority that allow them to accomplish great things. There are virtually no documented instances of troubled schools being turned around without intervention by a powerful leader. Many other factors may contribute to such turnarounds, but leadership is the catalyst (Leithwood, Louis, Anderson, & Wahlstrom, 2004).

Roles and Responsibilities

The Intern

Each intern is responsible for completing his or her required internship hours and for developing, participating in, documenting, and reflecting on his/her internship experiences throughout the program. Intern responsibilities include the following:

- Discuss the internship scope and responsibilities and how to initiate the internship with his/her university advisor prior to beginning.
- Initiate a meeting with his/her school internship supervisor to discuss the internship scope and responsibilities and develop an internship program plan.
- Draft an initial internship program plan to be reviewed and approved by his/her program advisor and internship supervisor.
- Engage in all tasks and responsibilities outlined in the plan, while being available for leadership development opportunities throughout the internship.
- Maintain a log and reflective journal on all internship activities.
- Set high standards/expectations.
- Connect research/theory and practice.
- Provide a service to the district/school.
- Develop a global perspective.
- Meet regularly with internship supervisor and university advisor throughout the internship to discuss observations and hands-on learning experiences, gain feedback on internship responsibilities and work, and be assessed on leadership knowledge and skills.
- Produce internship documentation, reflections, and reports as required by the university.

All interns are expected to demonstrate professional conduct and integrity throughout the entire internship experience and program. They are to keep sensitive information confidential, take initiative in guiding their internship experience, maintain clear communication with their school and district internship supervisors and program advisor, and generally behave in a professional manner.

How challenging your internship experience will be, to a great extent, is up to you. Like the old adage, "You get out of it what you put into it," you are urged to raise the bar and seek a true challenge for several very important reasons. First, you will be observed during your experience and others will clearly see the rigor and expectations you set for yourself. Second, while being an intern, there may be no other time when so many leaders will take the time to teach, counsel, and assist in your learning, development, and practice. Third, the day will come when you are standing in front of a group of very bright, educated, and experienced adults "expecting" to see a confident and competent leader. The internship is the opportunity to build the confidence and competence for that day. And finally, throughout a leadership career, you can positively affect the lives of thousands of students.

This text will serve as a guide for developing, monitoring, maximizing, and evaluating your planned experience. It differs greatly from previous internships where the prospective leader waited for assigned tasks or was given a limited range of opportunity to grow and develop. Now, you will be challenged to begin skill development toward mastery of national and state standards for educational leaders. While practicing and assessing levels of knowledge, skill, and dispositions of each standard, you will incorporate theory and lessons from previous or concurrent courses in leadership and management.

You will develop, refine, improve, and incorporate these skills into your repertoire, along with gaining new knowledge and mindsets in a vast spectrum of school contexts. Examples of the differing contexts are staff development, classroom instruction, budgeting, transportation, food service, technology, and others that will make up the 45 activity areas (Section 2.1). In addition to the 45 areas to show progress in mastery of State and national standards are critical skills "beyond the standards" (Section 2.2). You are strongly advised to incorporate as many of these activities as possible in your internship plan. Your plan will need to be approved by the university and school supervisor.

You will meet and learn from a wide variety of individuals, such as the personnel director, athletic director, principal, superintendent, board member, and parents and leaders in the community, etc. Your reputation can move from a skilled and competent teacher to a skilled and competent leader. We are depending on your leadership to better educate the next generation of our society.

University Advisor

The university advisor provides collegial and individual support to his or her assigned intern throughout the internship. The advisor facilitates ongoing reflection that leads to a deeper understanding by the interns of the assumptions and values that they bring to these roles, as well as of their personal leadership styles, practices, and the ways that values, style, and practices are intertwined:

- The advisor helps to develop each intern's plan at the beginning of the internship.
- The advisor meets formally with each intern either one-on-one, in small groups (such as conference groups), or in whole-group seminars throughout the internship period. During these sessions, the advisor encourages intern reflection on the leadership role and

work, facilitates discussions of internship challenges and leadership strategies, and fosters leadership development generally.

♦ The advisor meets with each intern on-site periodically throughout the internship. During the on-site visits, the advisor observes the intern in his/her work and consults with the site supervisor to ensure that the internship experiences are varied, appropriate, and in keeping with the intern's internship plan. The advisor provides written or oral feedback to the intern.

♦ The advisor monitors each intern's field experiences using the logs and reflective journal. The advisor should evaluate the breadth and depth of the intern's work, using the ELCC/NELP standards or other standards as a framework in reviewing intern hours. Using this information, the advisor can provide regular feedback and guidance as appropriate.

♦ The advisor meets regularly with the intern and internship supervisor to discuss the internship content and the intern's leadership opportunities for independent work, address problems and challenges, and identify new learning priorities.

♦ The advisor is available to the intern and internship supervisor by phone and email for problem solving and guidance.

♦ The advisor provides the intern evaluative feedback at the end of the internship experience.

School Building Internship Supervisor

The school building internship supervisor is typically the intern's principal or assistant principal. He or she assigns the internship work, supervises the intern, and coordinates the intern's work. The school building internship supervisor functions as a role model, supervisor, coach, and mentor throughout the intern's experience. The supervisor guides the intern, challenging him or her to grow as an educational decision maker, instructional leader, and manager of a complex organization.

The school internship supervisor should have a demonstrated record of effective educational leadership, particularly as outlined by the ELCC/NELP standards; have the time and interest to supervise the intern throughout the internship period; and be committed to the program's vision of educational leadership and its role in developing quality leadership in interns. Finally, the school internship supervisor should support a developmental approach to mentoring the intern, from providing exposure and orientation to promoting independence and responsibility.

The school internship supervisor's responsibilities include the following:

♦ Meet with the intern initially to discuss the internship scope and the intern's responsibilities throughout the internship.

♦ Meet with the intern regularly (at least weekly) to discuss his/her responsibilities, progress, and leadership learning experiences, as well as to provide guidance and assistance in helping the intern and feedback as needed.

- Provide the intern with exposure to various building-level leadership experiences.
- Provide the intern with developmental leadership experiences, with graduated responsibility and leadership.
- Orient the intern to school leadership as a career and provide coaching on the job search and interview process, as well as advice on transitioning from teaching to leading careers.
- Meet with the intern and university advisor intermittently to review the intern's progress and discuss the internship experience.
- Provide formal feedback and assessment of the intern's work and leadership development at the end of the internship.

Recommended Mentoring Practices

- *New challenges.* Be mindful of interns' strengths and encourage them to take on responsibilities that are "outside of their comfort zone."
- *Wide exposure.* Provide exposure to a wide range of leadership experiences through shadowing and co-participation at meetings inside and outside the school or district. Couple shadowing and co-participation with reflective conversations.
- *Buddying.* Create an informal buddy system and foster networking by pairing the intern with another new administrator.
- *Weekly meeting.* Schedule a weekly time to meet with the intern (i.e., first thing in the morning or end of the day on Friday) to debrief on the week's experiences, internship experiences, and other matters. Hold this time as "sacred."
- *Learning walks.* Conduct learning walks of a department with the intern and encourage him/her to provide reflections and to think about how to provide feedback to the teachers based on observations.
- *Experiencing the practice of other leaders.* Expose interns to other leadership styles in and outside the school and district, and follow up with reflective conversations about situational leadership and differences in approaches.
- *Presentation opportunities.* Arrange for interns to make small- and large-group presentations such as at a faculty meeting, committee meeting, PTA meeting, or board of education meeting.
- *Discussion of personal matters.* Use personnel and student matters (while respecting confidentiality) as mini case studies for talk-aloud problem solving and reflection.
- *Public support.* Be aware of how interns are presented publicly, so that other staff will take their contributions seriously.
- *Provision of learning opportunities at other schools.* Arrange for leadership learning opportunities at other school levels.

- ♦ *Balance.* Encourage discussion about the whole person, so interns can explore issues of work, family, and career balance.
- ♦ *Use of interns as a resource.* Take advantage of opportunities to engage interns in supporting the implementation of initiatives and evaluation of gaps or differences in utilization.
- ♦ *Transition.* Review interns' existing school and district responsibilities and redirect their work as appropriate (particularly to wind down prior or existing committee work and to take up new responsibilities).
- ♦ *Group process.* Give interns more opportunities to work with various groups, so they can learn more about multiple needs and perspectives and how to balance them.

Assessing the Intern and Field Experiences

Key to learning in the internship is assessment and feedback from self, peers, supervisors, and university faculty. It is highly recommended that interns and their programs use state and national standards as frameworks for intern assessment. These standards define the field's expectations for quality leadership, are usually the basis for program content, and are often the basis for evaluating school leader practice. Thus, using these standards in internship assessment fosters coherence and supports ongoing professional learning in the program and beyond.

Candidate assessment in the internship occurs at three stages throughout the experience. These include:

Stage One: Intern self-assessment and readiness, determining skill needs and priorities as a basis for planning in Stage 2.

Stage Two: Collaboration with school and university supervisors to reach consensus and final approval of the internship plan. Adjusting plans to take advantage of new opportunities or address unforeseen problems that arise. Supervisors should guide and support appropriate changes to the initial internship plan.

Stage Three: Monitoring progress in the implementation of the internship, using logs and reflections and soliciting feedback from peers, supervisors, and faculty. Program faculty are encouraged to monitor the following throughout each candidate's internship, using the intern's logs, reflections, and discussions:

- ♦ Leadership identity formation – How is the intern's understanding and identity with school leadership developing?
- ♦ Breadth and depth on leadership skills and practices – Does the intern have enough experiences in each standard?
- ♦ Depth – Has the intern's leadership skills developed in depth in one or more standards areas? Has the intern achieved independence as a leader in one or more skill area?

Stage Four: Evaluation. Program faculty will look across all the evidence that interns have provided to make a summative assessment about the candidate's readiness for program completion and advancement to an initial school leader position. Program faculty should use a standards-based rubric to evaluate interns' portfolios of proficiencies and accomplishments and action research or other leadership projects. Where possible, each intern's portfolio and project should be evaluated by two or more scorers, ideally independent of the program. Program faculty should also gather the following information as part of evaluating an intern's performance:

- Feedback from internship supervisor about the intern's performance and leadership readiness.
- Intern self-assessment of skills, dispositions, and leadership orientation.
- Interns' career advancement intentions and transitions.
- State licensure assessment results.

Outline of the Internship

Stage One: Assessment
- Choose the school/district site and supervisor.
- Develop the vita.
- Complete the Dispositions and Standards Assessment.
- Review other assessments and evaluations.
- Obtain and analyze school/district assessments, improvement plans, etc.
- Analyze assessments for areas needing improvement and a priority of focus.

Stage Two: Plan
- Choose activities from each of the 45 skill areas to meet professional standards.
- Choose activities from skill areas beyond the standards (Section 2.2, items 46–52).
- Include any required activities assigned by the university supervisor.
- Choose initial dispositions and interpersonal skills to improve (others added later).
- Meet with site supervisor to reach consensus on the planned activities and plan local project(s) and various service activities.
- Decide which individuals to work with, observe, and interview, and compile a networking list of these contacts.
- Organize the portfolio used to document the internship.
- Present the overall plan to university supervisor, if applicable.

Stage Three: Implementation
- ♦ Implement planned activities and be open to new opportunities.
- ♦ Develop the 12 essential competencies of leadership.
- ♦ Monitor and improve dispositions and interpersonal skills.
- ♦ Reflect in and on practice and keep a reflective journal.
- ♦ Keep a log of activities.
- ♦ Monitor progress toward mastery of state and national standards.
- ♦ Adjust intern activities throughout this stage.

Stage Four: Evaluation
- ♦ Complete final log and portfolio.
- ♦ Document progress toward mastery of national and/or state standards.
- ♦ Summarize key learning from experience in reflective practice, social justice, ethical and critical reasoning, and disposition/ interpersonal skill and fundamental skill development.
- ♦ Complete the action research or project report.
- ♦ Compile a prioritized list of school/district improvements and recommendations.
- ♦ Update the vita (include Principal Intern position), compose letter of application, and develop a future professional development plan.
- ♦ Present the Final Internship Report to the site supervisor and/or university supervisor.

The Developmental Nature of the Internship

The internship is a multifaceted learning process in which candidates integrate theory with practice by learning and practicing the craft of educational leadership. Through a series of leadership development experiences in an apprenticeship-like process, candidates develop leadership skills and a career orientation, assess their commitment to a career in the field, and receive feedback on their developing leadership knowledge, skills, and performance.

The internship, while site specific, is typically designed in accordance with national and state school leadership standards and the guidelines for an internship: Candidates demonstrate the ability to accept genuine responsibility for leading, facilitating, and making decisions typical of those made by educational leaders. The experience(s) should provide interns with substantial responsibilities that increase over time in amount and complexity and involve direct interaction and involvement with staff, students, parents, and community leaders.

Level 1: Observing. At this initial level, candidates' leadership development begins with job shadowing and exposure activities. This internship stage begins the intern's organizational socialization, fostering role clarification,

Table 1 Levels and Scope of Development for Interns

Level 1	Level 2	Level 3	Level 4
Observing	*Participating*	*Initial Leading*	*Independent Leading*
			Becoming more independent in leadership responsibilities
		Taking responsibility for leadership tasks, with oversight	
	Assisting and collaborating in leadership tasks		
Being exposed to leadership work			

with exposure to school functions and operations from a leader's perspective (Browne-Ferrigno, 2003; Brody, Vissa, & Weathers, 2010). It also begins the intern's leadership identity development, shifting from teacher to leader perspective (Browne-Ferrigno, 2003; Crow, 2012). Internship activities might be shadowing a principal or assistant principal for a day or week, attending leadership team meetings and committee meetings as an observer, and exploring the school's community to learn more about its context. Candidates can also visit various nonacademic school departments, services, and operations (such as the front office, transportation, maintenance, food services, and support services) to observe work first hand, interview supervisors and staff about their responsibilities, and learn how all school systems are connected and coordinated. This initial stage, of only observing, should be brief, but some leadership exposure activities – such as attending leadership team meetings – could be incorporated throughout the internship.

Level 2: Participating. At the second stage, interns would begin to participate in leadership work, assisting other school leaders in supervision and management. The intern is exposed to how to perform an array of leadership tasks by working alongside his or her supervisor or mentor. Lave and Wenger (1991) term this stage as learning through peripheral participation (Lave & Wenger, 1991). Williams, Matthews, and Baugh (2004) apply this concept to the internship by describing this learning process as both doing and observing, in which interns co-participate with their supervisors in completing part of a leadership task while simultaneously observing how their supervisors perform the work (Williams et al., 2004). Typically, developmental leadership experiences at this stage are operational tasks, such as performing bus, playground, and lunchtime supervision duties, assisting with professional development sessions or faculty meetings, and preparing data analyses and reports. Interns are also simultaneously able to work with different school constituencies – students, teachers, other staff, parents and families, and community members – gaining insight into leadership responsibilities and perspectives. This stage, while longer than the first, should be transitional, leading to more independent leadership work in the next two stages.

Level 3: Initial Leading. At the third level, interns begin to take independent responsibility for portions of leadership work, while being closely guided and supervised. Darling-Hammond, Meyerson, and others (2010) describe this type of internship experience as "engaging in leadership responsibilities for sustained periods of time under the tutelage of expert veterans" (Darling-Hammond et al., 2010, p. 182). This is the longest phase, during which interns have opportunities to conduct leadership work across core domains of responsibility, such as those defined by national standards (National Policy Board for Educational Administration, 2015), while being closely supervised by their school leader or internship supervisor. Interns' work resembles on-the-job training, in which interns develop skills through real work experience. During this phase, interns are coached in how to perform their leadership work and encouraged to make connections to coursework, while deepening their leadership identity and skills (Shoho, Barnett, & Martinez, 2012).

Level 4: Independent Leading. At this fourth level, interns take even more independent responsibility for leadership work, with little guidance and supervision. At this stage, interns are primarily mentored, rather than coached, to reinforce and deepen their leadership skills (Crow, 2012). Interns are likely to work independently on discrete projects or problems of practice, gaining depth in their experience, rather than striving for breadth across areas of work (Browne-Ferrigno & Muth, 2006). This work moves the intern from the stage of peripheral participation to central participation, enacting school leader work as would be more typical for a beginning school leader. This work is likely to occur during the latter part of the intern's experience and allows him/her to demonstrate new acquired leadership skills and practices and will likely yield accomplishments that can serve as exemplars of skill proficiency when pursuing new positions.

Meeting Professional Standards

Educational leaders must be very familiar with the standards of performance that guide their profession. The text is designed to meet these standards set by the National Policy Board for Educational Administration. This board is made up of the following professional organizations:

American Association of Colleges for Teacher Education (AACTE)
American Association of School Administrators (AASA)
Council for the Accreditation of Educator Preparation (CAEP)
Council of Chief State School Officers (CCSSO)

National Association of Elementary School Principals (NAESP)
National Association of Secondary School Principals (NASSP)
National Board for Professional Teaching Standards (NBPTS)
National Council of Professors of Educational Administration (NCPEA)
University Council for Educational Administration (UCEA)

The standards were designed to identify and establish a set of common professional standards for school leaders. It was felt that a set of common standards would provide an avenue for improvement efforts in a variety of areas of administrative leadership. "The standards set out to improve school leadership by improving the quality of programs that prepare school leaders while establishing a level of accountability of the efforts of these programs" (Murphy, Shipman, & Pearlman, 1997). The standards have been adopted in 44 states. This is due to its quality, comprehensiveness, and acceptance by many of our nation's leading school administrative organizations and accrediting agencies. The new millennium has ushered in a sense of working cooperatively to better prepare school leaders (NCPEA, 2000).

The NPBEA's Professional Standards for Educational Leaders 2015 set high benchmarks for the educational leader to meet (National Policy Board for Educational Administration, 2015). Many are standards that can only be fully mastered following full-time administrative positions. The internship, however, will be the beginning experience for meeting the standards. The ten standards, described in detail in Appendix C, expect the aspiring administrator to:

- Create a mission, vision, and core values
- Act with ethics and professional norms
- Strive for equity and cultural responsiveness
- Develop intellectually rigorous curriculum, instruction, and assessment
- Cultivate a community of care and support for students
- Develop the professional capacity of school personnel
- Foster a professional community for teachers and staff
- Engage families and community
- Manage operations and management
- Support continuous school improvement

Leadership preparation programs that want or are required to be nationally accredited must align their program content and internships to the Educational Leadership Constituent Council (ELCC) leadership preparation standards (Educational Leadership Constituent Council, 2011). The internship standard states that a building-level education leader applies knowledge that promotes the success of every student through a substantial and sustained educational leadership internship experience that has school-based field experiences and clinical internship practice within a school setting and is monitored by a qualified, on-site mentor (Educational Leadership Constituent Council, 2011).

This eleventh standard includes criteria for the form and nature of the internship, including that the internship experience

- provide for significant experience in a school content wherein interns can apply their content knowledge and develop their leadership skills;
- be of sufficient duration, for at least six months, with a concentration of 9–12 hours per week; and
- provide quality on-site mentoring from an experienced school leader.

Interns should be aware of these program standards and review with their program advisor their programs' approach to meeting these standards and how they shape internship opportunities and expectations.

The intern should also be knowledgeable of the differing professional associations that provide the guidance and resources for effective school leadership. Although supportive of the Professional Standards for Educational Leaders 2015, each association may offer additional standards, competencies, proficiencies, and other resources to assist school leaders in a particular field. It is strongly recommended that the intern become an active member in the professional associations of his/her choice for continued and further professional development. Appendices C–F list the standards and/or proficiencies for these associations.

Additionally, the intern should review their respective state standards to ensure that the intern plan activities meet these requirements also. Keep in mind that most state licensure exams are based on state standards rather than national standards, although most overlap and the similarities are much greater than any minor differences. Typically, state standards address all of the national standards and either add a few additional ones or elaborate on some details of a standard.

Internship Assessment

The first step is to develop a plan for individual improvement and this plan should be based on a diagnosis of your strengths and improvement needs. There are many tools available to assist you with this diagnosis. You should also incorporate feedback you've received from mentors and coaches into the development of this plan. Once your development plan is complete, you must link the realities of the internship venue to your plan. Too often, we see development plans that aren't connected to the school improvement plan. In order to provide you the meaningful developmental experiences, your plan must align with the school improvement plan.

In this part, the intern must gather and analyze various personal and district/school documents. These include a current vita, Professional Standards for Educational Leaders 2015 self-assessment, dispositions assessment, other self-assessments and evaluations, and district/school improvement and/or strategic plans. The intern will also compile a list of available resources. The following sections further explain the needed documentation. The final section provides guidelines for analysis and reporting.

1.1 Vita

The intern should complete a draft of his/her vita during the assessment phase of the internship. A vita lists the facts of education, experience, and accomplishments. It can be used for learning and planning the internship and future professional development. The vita should be reviewed to note knowledge, experience, and accomplishments in specific leadership areas, as well as inexperience in other areas. The internship experience should be cited and added to the vita at the end of the internship. A sample vita and guidelines for the vita development are listed in Appendix A.

1.2 Self-Assessment of NPBEA's Professional Standards for Educational Leaders 2015

The standards set by the National Policy Board for Educational Administration (NPBEA) include ten areas that school administrators are expected to master as they lead their schools. Although complete mastery can only come from extended experience in the position, interns are expected to be cognizant of these professional goals. Review the standards in Appendix C and note particular standards in greatest need for focus in the internship plan. Reflections and documentation of progress toward all standards will be required at the end of the internship.

1.3 Self, Peer, and Supervisor's Assessment of Dispositions

It's important to know yourself and know how others view you. This activity is designed to assess your dispositions in a number of areas. Some readers may be unfamiliar with the use of the term *disposition*. Disposition, in this context, describes a person's inclination to do something.

Dispositions are rooted in deeply held beliefs, values, and previous experiences. Successful leaders understand why they behave the way they do: They are aware of the beliefs and experiences that have shaped their current practice. Because successful leaders strive for a mutual understanding between themselves and those they serve, they often seek feedback from peers, superiors, and subordinates.

Make copies of the following disposition assessment. This dispositions assessment was derived from previous 2001 standards. The new policy standards do not include dispositions, but the authors believe in the importance of knowing and understanding your educational leadership dispositions. Distribute a copy to a peer and a superior. Complete one copy of the evaluation yourself. Then compare the results of your self-assessment with the assessments made by others. Use your results to assist in the development of your internship plan.

Dispositions Assessment

Please circle the indicator that you believe most accurately describes evidence of the following dispositions. This is not a recommendation form on the merit or expertise of the person, but an assessment of your perspective of the beliefs behind the words and/or actions of the person. Please complete this assessment as accurately and honestly as possible. Thank you for your time and effort.

SE (strong evidence)   LE (limited evidence)   NS (not seen)   OE (opposing evidence)

The intern believes in, values, and is committed to:

1) The educability of all	SE	LE	NS	OE
2) A school vision of high standards of learning	SE	LE	NS	OE
3) Continuous school improvement	SE	LE	NS	OE

4) The inclusion of all members of the school community   SE   LE   NS   OE

5) Ensuring that students have the knowledge, skills, and values needed to become successful adults   SE   LE   NS   OE

6) A willingness to continuously examine one's own assumptions, beliefs, and practices   SE   LE   NS   OE

7) Doing the work required for high levels of personal and organizational performance   SE   LE   NS   OE

8) Student learning as the fundamental purpose of schooling   SE   LE   NS   OE

9) The proposition that all students can learn   SE   LE   NS   OE

10) The variety of ways in which students can learn   SE   LE   NS   OE

11) Lifelong learning for self and others   SE   LE   NS   OE

12) Professional development as an integral part of school improvement   SE   LE   NS   OE

13) The benefits that diversity brings to the school community   SE   LE   NS   OE

14) A safe and supportive learning environment   SE   LE   NS   OE

15) Preparing students to be contributing members of society   SE   LE   NS   OE

16) Making management decisions to enhance learning and teaching   SE   LE   NS   OE

17) Taking risks to improve schools   SE   LE   NS   OE

18) Trusting people and their judgments   SE   LE   NS   OE

19) Accepting responsibility   SE   LE   NS   OE

20) High-quality standards, expectations, and performances   SE   LE   NS   OE

21) Involving stakeholders in management processes   SE   LE   NS   OE

22) A safe environment   SE   LE   NS   OE

23) School operating as an integral part of the community   SE   LE   NS   OE

24) Collaboration and communication with families   SE   LE   NS   OE

25) Involvement of families and other stakeholders in school decision-making processes   SE   LE   NS   OE

26) The proposition that diversity enriches the school   SE   LE   NS   OE

27) Families as partners in the education of their children   SE   LE   NS   OE

28) The proposition that families have the best interests of their children in mind   SE   LE   NS   OE

29) Resources of the family and community needing to be brought to bear on the education of students   SE   LE   NS   OE

30) The right of every student to a free, quality education   SE   LE   NS   OE

31) Bringing ethical principles to the decision-making process   SE   LE   NS   OE

32) Subordinating one's own interest to the good of the school community   SE   LE   NS   OE

33) Accepting consequences for one's principles and actions   SE   LE   NS   OE

34) Using the influence of one's office constructively and productively in the service of all students and their families   SE   LE   NS   OE

35) Development of a caring school community   SE   LE   NS   OE

36) Education as a key to opportunity and social mobility   SE   LE   NS   OE

37) Recognizing a variety of ideas, values, and cultures   SE   LE   NS   OE

38) Using legal systems to protect student rights and improve student   SE   LE   NS   OE
    opportunities

Additional comments or elaboration on any of the above items:

_____

_____

_____

_____

_____

1.4 Other Assessments and Evaluations

The intern will gather and review other personal evaluations and assessments that are available. These can include:

- Recent annual performance evaluations
- NASSP Leadership Skills Assessment at www.nassp.org
- NAESP assessment material at www.naesp.org
- Myers-Briggs or Keirsey Temperament at www.keirsey.com
- True Colors
- The book *StrengthsFinder 2.0* by Tom Rath
- Other relevant assessments from workshops or university courses.

The intern should summarize the findings and note major strengths in knowledge, skill, disposition, and experience, as well as weaknesses and areas needing improvement.

1.5 District/School Assessment

The final assessment report must include current district/school needs. The intern should summarize and prioritize the major goals and needs for the district/school. These can be gathered from current documents such as:

- District/school improvement plans and needs assessments
- Strategic plans
- Mission statement
- Recent accreditation reports

- ◆ Action plans
- ◆ Other evidence of district/school needs or goals.

1.6 Assessment Summary

Following the compilation and analysis of the previously gathered information, the intern will prepare a summary for the overall plan report, which is given at the end of Stage Two. The summary should include highlights from the following:

Vita

Present a brief overview of the significant experiences and accomplishments in leadership, teaching, professional development, and service. The intern may use a narrative or bulleted format for the presentation.

Professional Standards for Educational Leaders 2015 Self-Assessment

Include a listing of the major areas of significant knowledge and experience, as well as the major areas of limited knowledge and experience. The intern is advised to begin collecting documentation of evidence supporting strengths and performance that meet each standard. Evidence collected at the present time should be included.

Dispositions Assessments

This should include a listing of major areas of consensus for having *strong evidence* of the disposition and areas of consensus for *not seen* and/or *opposing evidence* for the disposition. The intern should also note dispositions that differ between the self-assessment and either peer, supervisor, or subordinate assessments.

Other Evaluations and/or Assessments

Include a brief summary of recent past annual performance evaluations noting significant areas that relate to leadership and overall job performance. The intern should also provide summaries/highlights of other evaluative or assessment data.

District/School Needs Assessment

Include an overview of the current district/school improvement plans, strategic plans, needs assessments, and/or accreditation reports. This can be presented in either narrative or bullets, highlighting major goal and need areas. The intern should also note priorities for the upcoming school year.

Plan

Following the review of the assessment report, the intern will design the internship plan. Stage Two lists recommended or suggested activities, guidelines for service activities, planning a local project, and collaborating with school and university supervisors.

2.1 Standards, Leadership Areas, and Activities

The following standards, leadership areas, and activities are provided to assist the intern in the design of the internship. Under each standard, leadership areas essential to meeting the standard are provided. There are 45 leadership areas that the intern should include in his/her plan, unless circumstances warrant omitting one or more areas. The most common circumstance is when the intern has more than adequate previous experience in an area. Omissions of any area in the intern plan should be justified and approved by the university and/or school supervisor.

Under each leadership area are a set of suggested or recommended activities and a place to plan other activities. *The intern is NOT required do all of the activities listed. However, the intern should complete at least ONE activity for each leadership area.* You should choose activities that align with your indicated strengths and improvement areas. Remember, build on your strengths and manage your weaknesses. You should consider the school or district goals and align your efforts with these initiatives.

It is normal for the intern plan to vary in time and effort between the leadership areas. For example, the intern may spend three hours in the area of transporting students and 30 hours in scheduling to increase the personalization throughout the school or budgeting to find additional resources to aid remedial work in literacy and numeracy. The intent of this text is to provide the needed flexibility for the intern to address his/her individual needs, provide service to the district/school, and take advantage of present opportunities.

Listed at the end of each leadership area is the following activity:

♦ Other related activities approved by your supervisor, and/or service activities to district/school assigned by the supervisor, and/or activities that are part of a larger project.

Often, various needs and opportunities are present that allow for different activities than those suggested in each area. Usually, the supervising administrator will provide additional activities and seek the intern's assistance with current needs of the district/school.

Many activities cite the term "district/school." Interns may choose to gain experience in some areas at the district level. It is advisable for the intern to pencil in an "X" for the activities where he/she has a need and/or interest in gaining knowledge, skill, or improvement in a disposition. Following this, he/she should meet with the supervisor and collaborate on the final plan.

The final plan should have a significant percentage of *experiences in leading* versus observing, participating, or carrying out assigned tasks AND have a focus on *increased learning*, overall *school improvement*, and *developing self and others*.

Professional Standards for Educational Leaders 2015

Standard 1

Mission, Vision, and Core Values
Effective educational leaders develop, advocate, and enact a shared mission, vision, and core values of high-quality education and academic success and well-being of each student.

Skill and Performance Areas for Meeting Standard 1
1. Vision/Mission
2. Strategic Planning
3. Data Collection and Analysis
4. Effective Communication
5. Negotiating/Consensus Building
6. Collaborative Decision-Making

1. Vision/Mission

Place an "X" by the activity or activities below that are approved or required by your school and university supervisor as part of your intern plan. You must choose at least ONE activity in this area but a majority to all of the activities are recommended for maximum learning and experience.

☐ a) Analyze the school's vision/mission statement as it relates to the school's master schedule. Too often, schools have slogans and not a vision. A school's master schedule is where the vision is enacted. Determine if the vision statement is reflected in the reality of the master schedule. Provide a summary and recommendations and include in the portfolio.

☐ b) Review board policy on vision, mission, and educational goals. Evaluate the degree to which congruence exists between the district/school vision, mission, and goals. Interview district administrators, faculty, and staff and obtain their perspectives regarding the vision, mission, and goals. Assess the level of agreement among parties involved and the degree of similarity between what is stated "officially" and the actual practice in the district/school. Note policies and practices not aligned with the vision. List recommendations for greater alignment with the vision and include your recommendations in the portfolio.

☐ c) Review and compare two different district/school vision statements. Try to obtain these from two distinct types of districts/schools (i.e., rich/poor, urban/suburban/rural, regular/charter/private, etc.). Note strengths and weaknesses of each and make recommendations for your district/school. Include your recommendations in the portfolio.

☐ d) Invite relevant constituents, (e.g., students, parents, citizens) and lead this group to find consensus on the development of a district, school, or subunit vision statement. Include the final vision statement and any relevant learning from the process in the portfolio.

- ♦ Other related activities approved by your supervisor, and/or service activities to district/school assigned by the supervisor, and/or activities that are part of a larger project.

2. Strategic Planning

Place an "X" by the activity or activities below that are approved or required by your school and university supervisor as part of your intern plan. You must choose at least ONE activity in this area but a majority to all of the activities are recommended for maximum learning and experience.

☐ a) Lead a project to develop a strategic plan for increasing students' literacy by designing and implementing a school-wide cross-content literacy program. Include relevant persons, e.g., teachers, students, curriculum leaders, reading specialists, special educators, and administrators. Infuse other necessary skill areas such as vision, data collection and analysis, communication, etc. Include a summary of the project, results, and recommendations in the portfolio.

☐ b) Review the strategic plan for your district/school. Note personnel involved in the plan's development, implementation, and evaluation. Investigate support and concerns from the various parties involved. Include your findings and recommendations in the portfolio.

☐ c) Serve on the strategic development, monitoring, or evaluation team for your district/school. This will depend on the current stage of the plan. Log your time and duties as part of the team. Cite significant learning and recommendations in the portfolio.

☐ d) Review, compare, and contrast strategic plans from your district/school and another district/school. Note the goals and processes used to attain the vision. Include your comparison and recommendations in the portfolio.

☐ e) Develop a strategic plan for your chosen project. Include the plan in the portfolio.

 ♦ Other related activities approved by your supervisor, and/or service activities to district/school assigned by the supervisor, and/or activities that are part of a larger project.

3. Data Collection and Analysis

Place an "X" by the activity or activities below that are approved or required by your school and university supervisor as part of your intern plan. You must choose at least ONE activity in this area but a majority to all of the activities are recommended for maximum learning and experience.

☐ a) Review current requirements for your school under the Every Student Succeeds Act (ESSA). Review the district's collection procedures and data collected. Interview persons directly involved, i.e., curriculum director, principal, teachers, and students. Analyze the data collected and the perspectives from each of the persons above and compile a list of actions needed to meet ESSA guidelines.

☐ b) Review board policy and administrative regulations regarding data collection, assessment, and evaluation. Evaluate the degree to which the policy and/or administrative regulations are being implemented. Write a reflective statement about ways in which the leader would seek to improve compliance in this area. If no policy/administrative regulation is in place, review other district policy/regulations in this area. The intern will prepare a policy/administrative regulation proposal for board consideration. The proposed policy/regulation will be included in the portfolio.

☐ c) Review the ways in which assessment data is used to impact practice by the following: board of education, superintendent, faculty, staff, and community relations/information department. Write a reflective statement about how the leader would seek to improve the use of assessment data in the district/school. The reflective statements will be included in the portfolio.

   ♦ Other related activities approved by your supervisor, and/or service activities to district/school assigned by the supervisor, and/or activities that are part of a larger project.

4. *Effective Communication*

Place an "X" by the activity or activities below that are approved or required by your school and university supervisor as part of your intern plan. You must choose at least ONE activity in this area but a majority to all of the activities are recommended for maximum learning and experience.

☐ a) Review board policy and administrative regulations regarding how communications will be managed in the district/school. Assess the level of compliance with policy/regulations and write a reflective statement describing how you believe communications might be improved. Include the statement in the portfolio.

☐ b) Write a memo to the faculty relaying information needing to be disseminated by the district/school office. Survey several persons receiving the memo and obtain advice on its organization, clarity, and intent and any recommendations for improvement. Include the memo and survey results in the portfolio.

☐ c) Assist in conducting a faculty meeting and a staff development session. Survey a random sample of the participants for strengths and areas needing improvement from your presentation. Include the results of the survey in the portfolio.

☐ d) Choose two effective listening techniques, e.g., posing probing questions, body language, etc., and apply the techniques in a student and/or parent conference. Personally assess the effectiveness in soliciting communication from the student and/or parent. Include assessment in the portfolio.

☐ e) Review and analyze current policy and practices that provide a "student voice." Interview a sampling of students from a variety of informal ethnicity and socioeconomic groups and assess differing perspectives on how to effectively increase the rights of students to be heard. Provide a summary of results and recommended action in the portfolio.

☐ f) Review and critique the processes used by the district/school to monitor the ongoing communication between the district/school and faculty and parents. Include your critique in the portfolio.

☐ g) In leading your selected project, gather evaluative feedback on your ability and capacity in giving information, listening, receiving information, seeking information, and monitoring information. Include the feedback in the portfolio.

☐ h) Review the district/school policy for handling Freedom of Information Requests. Include the key points of the policy in the portfolio.

♦ Other related activities approved by your supervisor, and/or service activities to district/school assigned by the supervisor, and/or activities that are part of a larger project.

5. *Negotiating/Consensus Building*

Place an "X" by the activity or activities below that are approved or required by your school and university supervisor as part of your intern plan. You must choose at least ONE activity in this area but a majority to all of the activities are recommended for maximum learning and experience.

- [ ] a) Review board policy/administrative regulations. Assess compliance with policy/regulations. Assess the leadership culture in the school/district. How frequently is top-down leadership versus collaborative leadership used? Does the leadership style of the school/district leaders most often used comply with official policy or administrative regulation? Write a reflective statement discussing the appropriate use of both top-down leadership and collaborative leadership. Include the statement in the portfolio.

- [ ] b) Assist in the administrative side of planning and implementing negotiations with a teacher union or teacher representative group. Note effective practices in the planning and bargaining process. Include these practices and recommendations in the portfolio.

- [ ] c) Choose a current issue in the district/school. Use steps for issue resolution with a small group of concerned parties. Reach consensus for a plan to resolve the issue and/or a critique on areas where resolution failed. Include plan and critique in the portfolio.

- [ ] d) In leading your selected project, include the steps used in gaining consensus for your project plan. Include the steps and assessment of outcomes and areas for needed improvement in the portfolio.

    - ◆ Other related activities approved by your supervisor, and/or service activities to district/school assigned by the supervisor, and/or activities that are part of a larger project.

Standard 1

6. Collaborative Decision-Making

Place an "X" by the activity or activities below that are approved or required by your school and university supervisor as part of your intern plan. You must choose at least ONE activity in this area but a majority to all of the activities are recommended for maximum learning and experience.

☐ a) With permission of the superintendent or principal, observe a district cabinet, school administrative team meeting, or other meeting where the leader plans to use collaborative decision-making. Observe the leader's behavior in outlining goals/problem definition, seeking information, providing information, clarifying/elaborating, challenging viewpoints, diagnosing progress, and summarizing. Include the observations and recommendations for improvement in the portfolio.

☐ b) In any of the activities chosen where you will be leading a group, practice each of the group leadership tasks cited in the above activity (a). At the conclusion of the meeting, have the group members complete a critical review of your performance of each of the tasks. Include a summary of the evaluations and recommendations for improvement in the portfolio.

☐ c) Survey administrators, teacher leaders, and teachers to assess which areas they believe decisions should be reached collaboratively. Include in the survey the perceived level of interest, expertise, need for a high-quality decision, and support for the decision. Discuss the results of the survey with the principal and compare agreement or disagreement with the administrators' and teachers' beliefs and current practices. Include a summary and recommendations in the portfolio.

♦ Other related activities approved by your supervisor, and/or service activities to district/school assigned by the supervisor, and/or activities that are part of a larger project.

Professional Standards for Educational Leaders 2015

Standard 2

Ethics and Professional Norms

Effective educational leaders act ethically and according to professional norms to promote each student's academic success and well-being.

Skill and Performance Areas for Meeting Standard 2

7) Ethics
8) Local Norms and Expectations
9) Philosophy of Leadership
10) Interpersonal Relationships
11) History and Traditions of the School and Community
12) School Board Policy and Procedures/State and Federal Law

7. Ethics

Place an "X" by the activity or activities below that are approved or required by your school and university supervisor as part of your intern plan. You must choose at least ONE activity in this area but a majority to all of the activities are recommended for maximum learning and experience.

☐ a) Draft a list of the guiding principles for ethical behavior that currently drive your beliefs, behavior, and practices. Interview one school and one business/civic leader and solicit the principles that they employ. Compare and contrast the lists and any impact on increased learning and school improvement. Include the lists, comparisons, and recommendations in the portfolio.

☐ b) Meet with a group of school staff members, e.g., secretaries, clerks, etc., and discuss their perspectives of positive ethical behavior. Avoid any discussion of specific instances or persons that may be seen as unethical. Seek recommendations for policy changes, additional training, and/or consequences to ensure increased ethical practices by certified personnel. Include recommendations in the portfolio.

☐ c) Meet with a representative group of students. Solicit their beliefs and experience with ethical practices in the school or classroom. Using the student perspectives, make recommendations for ensuring greater ethical practices for all students and include in the portfolio.

☐ d) Following the completion of your local project, consider the ethical beliefs that guided each of your actions. Discuss these beliefs with others involved in the project. Include feedback and any recommendations in the portfolio.

☐ e) Provide evidence for demonstrating that you actually do what you *tell* others to do. For example, if you ask others to monitor and adjust their performances, show how you do this in your work. Include evidence in the portfolio.

♦ Other related activities approved by your supervisor, and/or service activities to district/school assigned by the supervisor, and/or activities that are part of a larger project.

Standard 2

8. Local Norms and Expectations

Place an "X" by the activity or activities below that are approved or required by your school and university supervisor as part of your intern plan. You must choose at least ONE activity in this area but a majority to all of the activities are recommended for maximum learning and experience.

☐ a) Obtain a copy of the job description and evaluation instrument used for the position of study. Analyze the correlation between the requirements listed in the job description and the performance standards of the evaluation. Copies of job description and evaluation and the analysis will be included in the portfolio.

☐ b) Review the above materials and interview one supervisor responsible for evaluation of the position of study. Determine the degree of subjectivity in the evaluation process and any additional criteria used in determining the final evaluation. A summary of the interview should be included in the portfolio.

☐ c) Gather and compile a list of current demands/goals that are being placed under the responsibility of the position of study. These may come from state or board mandate, strategic plan, campus improvement plan, or community concerns. Relate these goals to areas on the job description and evaluation. The list of demands/goals and their relation to job description and evaluation are to be included in the portfolio.

♦ Other related activities approved by your supervisor, and/or service activities to district/school assigned by the supervisor, and/or activities that are part of a larger project.

9. *Philosophy of Leadership*

☐ a) Ask two to three respected leaders to describe their personal philosophy of leadership. Consider the collected responses and your personal answers to the following:

- ◆ What do you hope to accomplish as an educational leader?
- ◆ What core values or beliefs will you bring to the position?
- ◆ What characteristics and/or previous experiences have led to success?
- ◆ What expectations will you set for yourself and others?
- ◆ What example do you hope to model for faculty, students, and community?

Write a one-page description of your philosophy of leadership that addresses the questions above and include in the portfolio. Note: This may also be used in the Letter of Application activity.

10. Interpersonal Relationships

Place an "X" by the activity or activities below that are approved or required by your school and university supervisor as part of your intern plan. You must choose at least ONE activity in this area but a majority to all of the activities are recommended for maximum learning and experience.

☐ a) Choose from the following list of interpersonal skills the ones you wish to develop in your internship. It is recommended that you choose two to four of them, but you may add others as you become proficient in your first choices.

- ◆ Converses with others in a positive and pleasant manner
- ◆ Avoids criticizing and values diverse opinions/perspectives
- ◆ Avoids interrupting others while speaking
- ◆ Acknowledges accomplishments of others
- ◆ Promptly gets back to others with concerns or needs
- ◆ Shares information, in a timely manner, with others that need to know
- ◆ Accepts criticism
- ◆ Avoids being defensive when challenged
- ◆ Shares self with others
- ◆ Seeks to know and understand others

Document the period of time spent in developing each skill. Provide a reflective self-assessment of your progress. If possible, have a peer evaluate your level of skill/progress. Compare with the self-assessment and include in the portfolio.

☐ b) When leading meetings, focus on the following skills:

- ◆ Encourages others to participate
- ◆ Acknowledges feelings and mood relationships within the group
- ◆ Eases tensions when they occur
- ◆ Attempts to resolve conflicts constructively
- ◆ Encourages consideration of varying perspectives
- ◆ Empathetic to others
- ◆ Shares responsibilities
- ◆ Practices effective listening skills

Distribute a brief evaluation to one or more of the meeting participants in regard to your skill level of the above list. Review the evaluation and reflect on the results. Include progress made and further needs.

- ◆ Other related activities approved by your supervisor, and/or service activities to district/school assigned by the supervisor, and/or activities that are part of a larger project.

11. History and Traditions of the School and Community

Place an "X" by the activity or activities below that are approved or required by your school and university supervisor as part of your intern plan. You must choose at least ONE activity in this area but a majority to all of the activities are recommended for maximum learning and experience.

☐ a) Find a retired educator or elderly community member and conduct an interview. Focus on the oral history of the community and school system. Note significant events that affect the district/school today. Include highlights of the interview in the portfolio.

☐ b) Write a story about the person you met in activity (a). Include biography, education, and his or her philosophy of practice. How do these connect? Include the story and answers in the portfolio.

☐ c) Review past school board agendas, reports, and/or minutes. Note significant events, policy changes, and recurring themes or concerns that impact the district/school today. Include a summary in the portfolio.

☐ d) Review the officially adopted curriculum in one area. Determine the philosophical base that underlies the curriculum. Cite any recommendations for inclusion of other philosophies that would better serve the needs of all students. Include your recommendations in the portfolio.

☐ e) In a project that you lead, cite any relevant historical background. List one or more significant educational philosophers that would support the project goal. This information will be included in the background section of the project report. Include the report in the portfolio.

♦ Other related activities approved by your supervisor, and/or service activities to district/school assigned by the supervisor, and/or activities that are part of a larger project.

12. *School Board Policy and Procedures/State and Federal Law*

Place an "X" by the activity or activities below that are approved or required by your school and university supervisor as part of your intern plan. You must choose at least ONE activity in this area but a majority to all of the activities are recommended for maximum learning and experience.

☐ a) Review the board policy manual. Interview the superintendent or an assistant superintendent and discuss the compilation and updating process of the manual and the role of the board in this process. Discuss major areas that affect school principals. A summary of the interview will be included in the portfolio.

☐ b) Attend as many board meetings as possible. Include the agenda and a list of outcomes/decisions pertaining to each agenda item in the portfolio.

☐ c) Review the board training requirements and the role of the superintendent in this process. A summary of requirements, process, and the superintendent's role will be included in the portfolio.

☐ d) Review the board policy manual and note any policies that you are unfamiliar with or believe the school might be out of compliance with. Discuss your findings with your site supervisor. Note significant learning from the discussion and/or recommendations for additional learning on your part. Also note any recommendations for the school to be in compliance. Include significant learning and recommendations in the portfolio.

♦ Other related activities approved by your supervisor, and/or service activities to district/school assigned by the supervisor, and/or activities that are part of a larger project.

Professional Standards for Educational Leaders 2015

Standard 3

Equity and Cultural Responsiveness

Effective educational leaders strive for equity of educational opportunity and culturally responsive practices to promote each student's academic success and well-being.

Skill and Performance Areas for Meeting Standard 3

13) Climate for Cultural Diversity
14) Cross-Content Literacy
15) Equity in Practice

13. *Climate for Cultural Diversity*

For purposes of this section, cultural diversity is viewed as encompassing all groups that have historically experienced discrimination based on a race/ethnicity, gender, sexual orientation, income, learning or language ability, or other reason. Interns should develop the skills of assessing and addressing the school's cultural diversity climate by evaluating resources and stakeholder concerns and developing and implementing an improvement plan.

Place an "X" by the activity or activities below that are approved or required by your school and university supervisor as part of your intern plan. You must choose at least ONE activity in this area but a majority to all of the activities are recommended for maximum learning and experience.

☐ a) Examine and evaluate the history and social studies books with regard to the heritage and values of gender and culturally diverse populations. A copy of the evaluation and recommendations will be included in the portfolio.

☐ b) Meet with members of the language arts and/or reading departments and examine the literature used with regard to gender, race, ethnicity, and other minority stereotyping. An analysis and recommendations will be included in the portfolio.

☐ c) Meet confidentially with one or more teachers of differing racial groups to assess their concerns and recommendations for a positive culturally diverse climate in the district/school. A summary and critique of the interview will be included in the portfolio.

☐ d) Meet confidentially with one or more students of differing racial groups to assess their concerns and recommendations for a positive culturally diverse climate in the district/school. A summary and critique of the interview will be included in the portfolio.

☐ e) Meet confidentially with one or more parents of differing racial groups to assess their concerns and recommendations for a positive culturally diverse climate in the district/school. A summary and critique of the interview will be included in the portfolio.

☐ f) Develop and implement a plan to promote cultural diversity in the district/school or classroom. A copy of the plan will be included in the portfolio.

♦ Other related activities approved by your supervisor, and/or service activities to district/school assigned by the supervisor, and/or activities that are part of a larger project.

14. Cross-Content Literacy

Place an "X" by the activity or activities below that are approved or required by your school and university supervisor as part of your intern plan. You must choose at least ONE activity in this area but a majority to all of the activities are recommended for maximum learning and experience.

☐ a) Survey each department or grade level to determine how they are infusing literacy into their instructional program. Note efforts to work with other departments or grade levels to strengthen cross-content collaboration and include in the portfolio.

☐ b) Propose an agenda item or items for a scheduled faculty meeting to give each department or grade level a brief time to present how they are infusing literacy into their instruction. Include the agenda and highlights of the discussion in the portfolio.

☐ c) Work with each department or grade level to determine if they have created the "academic vocabulary" for their respective discipline. Include any completed lists and progress toward the development in the portfolio.

♦ Other related activities approved by your supervisor, and/or service activities to district/school assigned by the supervisor, and/or activities that are part of a larger project.

Standard 3

15. *Equity in Practice*

Place an "X" by the activity or activities below that are approved or required by your school and university supervisor as part of your intern plan. You must choose at least ONE activity in this area but a majority to all of the activities are recommended for maximum learning and experience.

☐ a) Enact an equity audit (Skrla, McKenzie, & Scheurich, 2008). Collect and disaggregate findings according to gender, race/ethnicity, and socioeconomic status (free and reduced lunch) from the data from the following sources:

- ♦ State exam scores
- ♦ Grades and other academic indicators
- ♦ Honor rolls
- ♦ Participation in extracurricular activities
- ♦ Participation in academic support services
- ♦ Participation in school clubs and organizations
- ♦ Failure reports
- ♦ Discipline referrals
- ♦ Detention referrals
- ♦ Suspensions (in and out of school)

Create a spreadsheet noting numbers and percentages of differing students in each of the above data sources. Look for subgroup differences by grade, program, or content area.

☐ b) Using the data collected in the above activity, produce an equity analysis report. Highlight where gaps are most pronounced and where policies, practices, and support services appear to be in need of improvement.

☐ c) Present the findings to each department or grade level (or entire faculty) and engage one or more groups in root cause analysis, investigate solutions, and devise plans to reduce or eliminate any inequities found. Include the findings and plans in the portfolio.

☐ d) Facilitate the implementation of one proposed solution, documenting its impact on the initially identified gap.

☐ e) Audit the school staff's cultural sensitivity and awareness of diversity and tolerance using cultural competency surveys or interview guides (Bustamante, Nelson, & Onwuegbuzie, 2009).

☐ f) Promote staff's cultural competence through professional development, using survey results and the equity audit as foundational and various cultural competence protocols to facilitate learning through faculty meetings and professional development seminars (Singleton & Linton, 2005).

- ♦ Other related activities approved by your supervisor, and/or service activities to district/school assigned by the supervisor, and/or activities that are part of a larger project.

Professional Standards for Educational Leaders 2015

Standard 4

Curriculum, Instruction, and Assessment

Effective educational leaders develop and support intellectually rigorous and coherent systems of curriculum, instruction, and assessment to promote each student's academic success and well-being.

Skill and Performance Areas for Meeting Standard 4

16) Analyzing the Curriculum
17) School/Program Scheduling
18) Learning/Motivation Theory
19) Learning Technology
20) Evaluation of Student Achievement/Testing and Measurements

16. Analyzing the Curriculum

Place an "X" by the activity or activities below that are approved or required by your school and university supervisor as part of your intern plan. You must choose at least ONE activity in this area but a majority to all of the activities are recommended for maximum learning and experience.

☐ a) Analyze and compare the curriculum with recommendations from the following: elementary level – NAESP's *Leading Learning Communities, 2nd edition* (2008); secondary level – NASSP's *Breaking Ranks: A Comprehensive Framework for School Improvement* (2011). Cite areas that align with and need change to meet the recommendations from the appropriate book. Summarize findings and recommended actions and include in the portfolio. (Consider this for a project that would include other relevant knowledge and skill areas.)

☐ b) Review board policy and administrative regulations regarding curriculum development, implementation, management, and evaluation. Evaluate compliance with relevant federal (ESSA) and state laws and regulations, as well as local board policy. Write a reflective statement outlining ways in which supervision/management of curriculum matters can be improved and include in the portfolio.

☐ c) Select one subject or course curriculum. Note the problem being addressed when it was written. Compile a list of the curriculum writers. Note which persons served as a representative for teachers, the subject matter, students, learning theory, and community/state standards. Note whether any weaknesses in the curriculum are present due to lack of representation in any of these areas. Make recommendations and include in the portfolio.

☐ d) Interview persons involved in the implementation of a district/school curriculum. Describe the implementation process and note successes and concerns/problems with its implementation. Evaluate the process used and recommendations for improvements and include in the portfolio.

☐ e) Actively participate, if possible, or interview a person with experience in the textbook selection process. Include an overview of the process, evaluative criteria used, and recommendations for improvement in the portfolio.

☐ f) Evaluate the text and other reading materials for one course. Include the reading level (lexile level) and aspects of cultural diversity or gender bias. Include an evaluation and recommendations in the portfolio.

☐ g) Research the processes used for curriculum evaluation in the district/school. Evaluate the methods used, intervals of time, and degree of participation by teachers, students, and administrators. Include the evaluation and recommendations in the portfolio.

☐ h) Go to the website of the American Psychological Association and search for Learner-Centered Psychological Principles: A Framework (www. apa.org/ed/lcp.html). Apply these 14 principles to understanding the strengths and weaknesses of the instructional program at your department, school, or district. Include a reflective summary of your experience in the portfolio.

☐ i) Determine curricula that is utilizing technology to improve content and delivery. Include this information in the portfolio.

    ♦ Other related activities approved by your supervisor, and/or service activities to district/school assigned by the supervisor, and/or activities that are part of a larger project.

Standard 4

17. *School/Program Scheduling*

Place an "X" by the activity or activities below that are approved or required by your school and university supervisor as part of your intern plan. You must choose at least ONE activity in this area but a majority to all of the activities are recommended for maximum learning and experience.

☐ a) Analyze the district/school schedule and make recommendations for increased efficiency and meeting student needs. Determine what extent variation in time is being utilized. Present these findings to the person responsible for scheduling to discuss their feasibility and merit. The analysis, recommendations, and comments from the person responsible for scheduling will be included in the portfolio.

☐ b) Participate in the process of student class scheduling. A brief overview of the process and any recommendations will be included in the portfolio.

☐ c) Meet with the counselor or administrator responsible for changes in student class schedules. Discuss the number of changes, rationale for changes, and ramifications of the change. Examine ways to reduce changes and/or better meet student needs. Include a summary and recommendations in the portfolio.

☐ d) Observe the opening week of school or district activities and cite the issues and/or goals for such activities. Interview several teachers and/or students and compare the issues and goals from each perspective. Note major concerns from administration, faculty, and students. A summary and recommendations for improvement will be included in the portfolio.

☐ e) Obtain a copy of school year closing procedures. Interview several teachers and/or students and compare the issues and goals from their perspective. Note major concerns from administration, faculty, and students. A summary and recommendations for improvement will be included in the portfolio

♦ Other related activities approved by your supervisor, and/or service activities to district/school assigned by the supervisor, and/or activities that are part of a larger project.

18. Learning/Motivation Theory

Place an "X" by the activity or activities below that are approved or required by your school and university supervisor as part of your intern plan. You must choose at least ONE activity in this area but a majority to all of the activities are recommended for maximum learning and experience.

☐ a) Review methods used to encourage student motivation in the classroom. Read two articles from refereed journals on motivation strategies and discuss readings with selected administrators and faculty. Write a reflection on the topic and include in the portfolio.

☐ b) Survey a school faculty on methods used to motivate students. Survey a sample of students soliciting methods that motivate them to perform in school. Compare and contrast the two surveys. Include the comparison and recommendations in the portfolio.

☐ c) Meet with a group of similar subject-area or grade-level teachers and review the current curriculum and lesson plans. Compile the amount of traditional, behavioral, cognitive, and experiential learning objectives used. Solicit methods for utilizing more cognitive and experiential objectives in the curriculum and lesson plans. Include the compilation and recommendation in the portfolio.

☐ d) Meet with a group of teachers and assess the amount of teaching that is at each student's challenge level (Vygotsky's [1978] model). Solicit recommended methods for achieving more instruction at each student's challenge level. Include methods and recommendations in the portfolio.

☐ e) Compile a list of all options for student belonging that the school offers. These could include clubs, study groups, sports teams, and other formal and informal groups. Calculate the percentage of students that belong to one or more student groups. Meet with several students and brainstorm reasons why students choose to belong or not to belong. Seek recommendations for more students belonging. Include the list, percentages, and recommendations in the portfolio.

☐ f) Compile a list of all examples of student recognition (honor roll, National Honor Society, National Junior Honor Society, National Elementary Honor Society, Key Club, school letter jackets, most improved student awards, etc.) that the school practices. Calculate the percentage of students that receive some type of school recognition. Note the percentages of students receiving academic recognition versus athletic recognition. Survey a broad spectrum of teachers, students, and parents, elicit additional means of recognizing students, and include in the portfolio.

   ♦ Other related activities approved by your supervisor, and/or service activities to district/school assigned by the supervisor, and/or activities that are part of a larger project.

Standard 4

19. *Learning Technology*

Place an "X" by the activity or activities below that are approved or required by your school and university supervisor as part of your intern plan. You must choose at least ONE activity in this area but a majority to all of the activities are recommended for maximum learning and experience.

☐ a) Review board policies related to the use of email, interactive technologies such as Web 2.0 tools and beyond, software license agreements, webpage construction, access to the Internet, and other district/school technologies. Review the degree of compliance between board policy and the district technology plan, as well as the legal aspects regarding the use and implementation of various technologies. Record your findings and recommendations in the portfolio.

☐ b) Using school improvement data, select a particular area of curricular need. Gather information on present and future technologies used to support teaching and learning in this curriculum/subject area. Make recommendations for expanded use of technology, addressing costs, training, and current and future needs of the students. Write a synopsis of your findings and recommendations in the portfolio.

☐ c) Interview persons responsible for purchasing, supporting, or managing technologies used for instruction. How is the budget allocated for purchasing, supporting, or managing technology? Report your findings and recommendations in the portfolio.

☐ d) Observe the use of technologies in the classroom, library, and/or computer lab. Discuss the technology implementation in these areas with the librarian, technology facilitator, lab supervisor, or a classroom teacher and several students. Compare and contrast strengths and weaknesses given by students and adults with respect to accessibility, engagement, and other areas within the national/district/school technology plans. Provide a summary of your observations and recommendations in the portfolio.

☐ e) Identify an innovative technology for your school/district. In other words, describe what an outside observer would expect to see in a school setting where technology has been given high priority over a ten-year period. Include in this the student outcomes/behaviors that you want to see occurring and how this will enhance student learning. Next, develop an evaluation tool or instrument to help you determine the extent to which a given school measures up to this reference point. Finally, apply your instrument to the school/district where you are assigned as an intern, analyze results, and formulate recommendations. Summarize your findings and include in the portfolio.

☐ f) Review the Acceptable Use Policy for students with regards to the Bring Your Own Device or one-to-one computing movement. Write a plan to support teachers as they address implementation concerns for integrating technology. Include your plan in the portfolio.

☐ g) Examine a school or classroom that incorporates a blended learning model using multiple modalities for instruction. Explain the impact this model of teaching and learning can have on an organization. Devise a plan that will embrace a blended learning model of instruction. Develop your plan in the portfolio.

☐ h) Develop a plan for educating the school on digital citizenship and social media. Determine the resources necessary for ensuring the safety of students by researching COPPA – Children's Online Privacy Protection Act (www.coppa.org). Devise a plan that will educate teachers, parents, and students about online protection and include in the portfolio.

☐ i) Design a technology plan that allows students to bring their own technology (BYOT) to class for instructional purposes. Discuss how the school will educate students, parents, and teachers on Wi-Fi connectivity, allowable Internet activities, and online safety precautions. Describe ways teachers can incorporate technology to enhance learning. Include this plan in the portfolio.

☐ j) Design a technology plan that allows for one device per student for instructional purposes. Discuss how the school will educate students, parents, and teachers on Wi-Fi connectivity, allowable Internet activities, and online safety precautions. Describe ways teachers can incorporate technology to enhance learning. Include this plan in the portfolio.

☐ k) Create a professional development plan that will help teachers integrate technology into the core curriculum for teaching and learning. Create a timeline and select who and how your training will be facilitated. Develop your plan and record it in the portfolio.

♦ Other related activities approved by your supervisor, and/or service activities to district/school assigned by the supervisor, and/or activities that are part of a larger project.

20. *Evaluation of Student Achievement/Testing and Measurements*

Place an "X" by the activity or activities below that are approved or required by your school and university supervisor as part of your intern plan. You must choose at least ONE activity in this area but a majority to all of the activities are recommended for maximum learning and experience.

☐ a) Review board policy and assess degree of compliance with board policy and educational plan. Discuss curriculum and assessment of student achievement with administrators and faculty. Write a reflective statement regarding ways that evaluations and assessment of student achievement might be improved. Include assessment of compliance and recommendations in the portfolio.

☐ b) Select one subject or course curriculum. Review the distribution of grades for the subject or course. Devise, distribute, and collect a brief needs assessment relating to strengths and concerns of the testing procedures and grading policy used. A copy of the assessment and recommendations for improving student performance and assessment will be included in the portfolio.

☐ c) Gather and analyze the district/school, state, and national normed test results. Assess the current strengths and weaknesses in student achievement. Make recommendations for improvement in student performance on standardized tests. Include the assessment and recommendations in the portfolio.

☐ d) Form and lead a team of teachers to study and develop a plan for improving test scores. The area chosen should be an area identified as a weakness in school achievement. The plan should be feasible, but may require additional funds and/or a broader base of support for its implementation. Include the plan and an overview of the team process in the portfolio.

☐ e) Randomly select a group of students and elicit their recommendations for how to improve preparation for tests. Compile and critique the student recommendations and address the issue of student input into this process. The critique and recommendation for student input will be included in the portfolio.

☐ f) Lead a group of common subject and/or grade-level teachers in the development and use of a six- or nine-week departmental/grade level exam. After administering the exam, meet with the teachers and discuss the merits of this type of testing for teachers and students. Include a brief log of activities, group process used, results of your leadership, and recommendations for the use of this type of testing in the portfolio.

   ♦ Other related activities approved by your supervisor, and/or service activities to district/school assigned by the supervisor, and/or activities that are part of a larger project.

Professional Standards for Educational Leaders 2015

Standard 5

Community of Care and Support for Students

Effective educational leaders cultivate an inclusive, caring, and supportive school community that promotes the academic success and well-being of each student.

Skill and Performance Areas for Meeting Standard 5

21) Supervision of Co-Curricular Education
22) Student Discipline
23) Student Services
24) Special Populations
25) Remediation Strategies

21. *Supervision of Co-Curricular Education*

Place an "X" by the activity or activities below that are approved or required by your school and university supervisor as part of your intern plan. You must choose at least ONE activity in this area but a majority to all of the activities are recommended for maximum learning and experience.

☐ a) Review board policy and evaluate school compliance with policy in the following areas: Coaches and sponsor assignments and rate of pay approved by the board on an annual basis; activities in compliance with federal law (Title IV); medical emergency plan in place and supervision plan implemented; insurance requirements complied with; and evaluation of personnel and programs in place. Discuss the conduct of co-curricular activities with administration, faculty, staff, and students. Explore perspectives of each group and write a reflection paper with recommendations that might improve the quality of experience the district/school provides for the benefit of students. Include the paper in the portfolio.

☐ b) Select an area of interest involving co-curricular activities. With the approval of the sponsor, assist in the planning and supervising of the activity. A critique of the learning experience for the students involved will be included in the portfolio. The critique should also address student motivation, discipline, and performance and its relation to the overall education of the student.

☐ c) Collaboratively work with one teacher in the planning and supervising of a co-curricular activity. A critique of the learning experience, using the indicators listed in activity (a), will be completed and included in the portfolio.

☐ d) Meet with a group of randomly selected and representative students to discuss the strengths and weaknesses of co-curricular activities. Recommendations for improving/expanding the strengths of such activities into other subject areas will be listed and included in the portfolio.

   ♦ Other related activities approved by your supervisor, and/or service activities to district/school assigned by the supervisor, and/or activities that are part of a larger project.

22. Student Discipline

Place an "X" by the activity or activities below that are approved or required by your school and university supervisor as part of your intern plan. You must choose at least ONE activity in this area but a majority to all of the activities are recommended for maximum learning and experience.

☐ a) Review board policy and school handbooks. Review current practice in the district/school. Meet and discuss discipline with administrators in charge of student discipline, faculty, staff, students, and selected parents. Assess district/school compliance with law (state and federal), policy, regulations, and student handbooks. Write a reflective statement on student discipline and include in the portfolio.

☐ b) Examine the district/school discipline policy and provide an analysis of its strengths and weaknesses. Include the analysis and recommendations in the portfolio.

☐ c) Review discipline referrals for a specific period and compile the data with regard to grade level, special education classification, race, and gender. A summary of the findings and recommendations for improvement will be included in the portfolio.

☐ d) Meet with a team for the Response to Intervention (RtI). Assess the current intervention procedures to support struggling learners. Who comprises the school team? How often do they meet? A summary of the meeting, major issues, and concerns and recommendations will be included in the portfolio.

☐ e) With permission of the administration, participate in a conference dealing with student discipline. Critique the session with regard to consequences imposed and the need for additional assistance with improving social skills. Include the critique and recommendations in the portfolio.

☐ f) Meet with a representative group of selected students to discuss school rules and discipline procedures. An analysis of the findings and recommendations for improvement will be included in the portfolio.

☐ g) Interview one administrator, one student, and a local law enforcement officer/school resource officer knowledgeable of current gang behavior. An analysis of these meetings with regard to current policy and efforts in the area will be completed and included in the portfolio.

- ♦ Other related activities approved by your supervisor, and/or service activities to district/school assigned by the supervisor, and/or activities that are part of a larger project.

23. *Student Services*

Place an "X" by the activity or activities below that are approved or required by your school and university supervisor as part of your intern plan. You must choose at least ONE activity in this area but a majority to all of the activities are recommended for maximum learning and experience.

☐ a) Review board policy regarding student services. Assess degree of compliance with policy and education plan. Identify ways student services might be improved and include in the portfolio.

☐ b) Participate in a career or educational program session with a counselor and a student. A critique of the session will be included in the portfolio.

☐ c) Interview a school nurse and discuss the major requirements, concerns, and goals for the school health program. Address issues such as AIDS, abuse, sex education, and any other current issues. A summary and recommendations will be included in the portfolio.

☐ d) Meet with the counselor, a member of the faculty or administration, and a parent to discuss the role of the school concerning children responding to their parents' divorce, single parents' needs, and after-school care. Concerns and recommendations will be included in the portfolio.

☐ e) Review policies related to dealing with bullying and lesbian, gay, bisexual, and transgender (LGBT) students. Determine if the school is in compliance with policy and assess whether practices within policy are effective in meeting student needs. A summary and recommendations will be included in the portfolio.

  ♦ Other related activities approved by your supervisor, and/or service activities to district/school assigned by the supervisor, and/or activities that are part of a larger project.

24. *Special Populations*

Place an "X" by the activity or activities below that are approved or required by your school and university supervisor as part of your intern plan. You must choose at least ONE activity in this area but a majority to all of the activities are recommended for maximum learning and experience.

☐ a) Meet with district/school pupil personnel staff to determine the degree of alignment of programs in the district for special populations with categories outlined in Perkins IV (Carl D. Perkins Career and Technical Education Improvement Act of 2006). These include:

   ♦ Individuals with disabilities
   ♦ Individuals from economically disadvantaged families, including foster children
   ♦ Individuals preparing for nontraditional training and employment
   ♦ Single parents, including single pregnant women
   ♦ Displaced homemakers
   ♦ Individuals with other barriers to educational achievement, including individuals with limited English proficiency

   Determine how the needs of special populations are being ascertained. Assess the effectiveness of the delivery system for addressing the needs. Include your assessment in the portfolio.

☐ b) Review requirements for the current Individuals with Disabilities Education Improvement Act (IDEIA) and meet with the special education director. Discuss responsibilities of principals in meeting the guidelines. Compile a list of recommendations principals will need to know and be able to do to meet IDEIA guidelines and better serve special education students. The list will be included in the portfolio.

☐ c) Attend one special education meeting involving initial placement or annual review. A critique of the meeting will be included in the portfolio.

☐ d) Interview a professional responsible for career and technical education. Major requirements, concerns, and goals for the program will be discussed. Summarize these issues and cite current and future plans to address these issues. The summary will be included in the portfolio with recommendations for improvement.

☐ e) Interview a professional responsible for the bilingual and/or ESL (English as a second language) program. Major requirements, concerns, and goals for the program should be discussed. Then observe a bilingual or ESL class and following the observation, discuss these issues with the teacher. A summary of the interview, observation, and discussion will be written and included in the portfolio.

Standard 5

☐ f) Interview professionals responsible for the gifted and at-risk programs. Note similarities and differences in goals, processes, and issues. Solicit recommendations that principals can employ to better meet the needs of both populations. A summary will be included in the portfolio.

☐ g) Accommodating students with disabilities is a permanent issue that is very often overlooked. After reviewing the Americans with Disabilities Act (ADA) materials, develop a plan for a successful accessible curriculum design in your school district when using technology to enhance instruction. Develop your plan and record it in the portfolio.

> ♦ Other related activities approved by your supervisor, and/or service activities to district/school assigned by the supervisor, and/or activities that are part of a larger project.

25. Remediation Strategies

Place an "X" by the activity or activities below that are approved or required by your school and university supervisor as part of your intern plan. You must choose at least ONE activity in this area but a majority to all of the activities are recommended for maximum learning and experience.

☐ a) Investigate all options for remediation from the research and interviews with the counselor, administration, department or grade-level chairs, curriculum and instruction department, other schools and districts, etc. The list should include but not limited to peer and cross-grade-level tutoring, after-school and summer school programs, study hall, in-class strategies, etc. Assess the effectiveness of options used and the rationale for not using other options. Present your findings to the faculty and elicit recommendations for improving remediation. Include the findings and recommendations in the portfolio.

☐ b) Interview a group (or individually) of representative students receiving remediation. Solicit students' perspectives on the value/success of the remediation and recommendations for improvement. Present your findings to the faculty and elicit recommendations for improving remediation. Include the findings and recommendations in the portfolio.

♦ Other related activities approved by your supervisor, and/or service activities to district/school assigned by the supervisor, and/or activities that are part of a larger project.

Standard 5

Professional Standards for Educational Leaders 2015

Standard 6

Professional Capacity of School Personnel

Effective educational leaders develop the professional capacity and practice of school personnel to promote each student's academic success and well-being.

Skill and Performance Areas for Meeting Standard 6

26) Supervision of Instruction/Instructional Strategies
27) Staff Development/Adult Learning
28) Personnel Procedures
29) Faculty and Staff Evaluation

26. *Supervision of Instruction/Instructional Strategies*

Place an "X" by the activity or activities below that are approved or required by your school and university supervisor as part of your intern plan. You must choose at least ONE activity in this area but a majority to all of the activities are recommended for maximum learning and experience.

☐ a) Conduct an audit to determine the degree to which the school or district has incorporated brain-based learning theory into the instructional program. Note what cognitive scientists provide that can assist a school or district and make recommendations for implementation and include in the portfolio.

☐ b) Visit the International Center for Leadership in Education (ICLE) website at icle.org and research their Rigor/Relevance Framework. Engage faculty and/or district staff in a discussion of the Rigor/Relevance Framework. Include a summary of the discussion, noting significant positions taken and perspectives elicited from the discussion in the portfolio.

☐ c) Conduct a book study with a department or grade-level faulty using *Mindset: The New Psychology of Success* by Carol Dweck. Include significant learnings and any results from the study in the portfolio.

☐ d) With permission of the principal and two teachers, conduct two classroom observations using the clinical supervision model, i.e., pre-conference, observation, analysis, and post-conference. Include a summary of the observation process and recommendations for improvement in the portfolio.

☐ e) Following each of the classroom observations and summaries above, complete the district teacher evaluation form for the two teachers (omit names). Note the differences between a clinical model (activity b) and the district evaluation form. Include the differences, recommendations, and copies of the completed forms in the portfolio.

☐ f) Observe one instructional assistant. Note duties, time, and expertise in academic assistance to the students. Include a summary of the observation and recommendations for improvement in the portfolio.

☐ g) Meet with a group of two instructional assistants and two teachers concerning the teacher evaluation process. Compile a list of strengths, weaknesses, and recommendations for improvement in the process. Discuss the role of the teachers and assistants in this process. Include critique and recommendations of the process and role in the portfolio.

☐ h) Select and administer two types of evaluation/observation instruments alternative to the official district form. Copies of the completed forms and recommendations for alternative evaluation forms will be included in the portfolio.

Standard 6

☐ i) Select one class to complete a student evaluation of the instruction and learning in their class. Summarize the data and meet with a group of students to discuss the strengths, weaknesses, and recommendations for using the process. Copies of the instrument, overview of the student meeting, and recommendations for student input in the process will be included in the portfolio.

☐ j) Interview one district-level instructional supervisor and assess current needs, goals, and level of service provided by central office instructional staff. Include the assessment and recommendations in the portfolio.

♦ Other related activities approved by your supervisor, and/or service activities to district/school assigned by the supervisor, and/or activities that are part of a larger project.

27. Staff Development/Adult Learning

Place an "X" by the activity or activities below that are approved or required by your school and university supervisor as part of your intern plan. You must choose at least ONE activity in this area but a majority to all of the activities are recommended for maximum learning and experience.

☐ a) Compile and analyze all policies and current practices by leaders that help in developing others. Interview administrators and faculty and assess the perceived effectiveness of current practices. Seek recommendations for greater efforts and results in developing others. Provide a summary of concerns and recommendations in the portfolio.

☐ b) Gather, from written evidence or from someone responsible for staff development, the yearly district/school staff development plan. The plan will be analyzed with respect to school mission, student achievement, and teacher evaluations. A copy or overview of the plan and its relationship to the above variables will be included in the portfolio.

☐ c) Collaborate with an experienced staff developer in one staff development activity. This activity should include planning, implementing, instructing, and evaluating. A copy of the agenda, relevant materials, and the evaluation will be included in the portfolio.

☐ d) Compile a list of all professional development activities completed by the faculty of a particular school. This should include activities provided by the district/school and outside of the district/school. Note discrepancies between the amount of professional development and the experience and subject areas of the teachers. Make recommendations for greater involvement in professional development by all faculty members. Include the list, patterns, and recommendations in the portfolio.

☐ e) Survey a broad spectrum of teachers to elicit recommendations for more effective and relevant professional development and assess the degree of importance that professional development should have in teacher evaluation. Include the survey results and recommendations for effective professional development and its use in teacher evaluation in the portfolio.

☐ f) Survey a broad spectrum of students to discover what they believe are the necessary areas of training for their teachers. Discuss the students' responses with the faculty and/or staff developers. Compare and contrast the perceived needs from the students with the current district/school staff development plan. Include the survey results, comparisons, and recommendations in the portfolio.

◆ Other related activities approved by your supervisor, and/or service activities to district/school assigned by the supervisor, and/or activities that are part of a larger project.

Standard 6

28. *Personnel Procedures*

Place an "X" by the activity or activities below that are approved or required by your school and university supervisor as part of your intern plan. You must choose at least ONE activity in this area but a majority to all of the activities are recommended for maximum learning and experience.

☐ a) Interview a person responsible for district personnel. Major requirements and issues to be discussed should include the planning, recruitment, selection, induction, compensation, evaluation, and dismissal of personnel. A summary of the interview will be included in the portfolio.

☐ b) Determine district plans to recruit and hire teachers that reflect underrepresented groups of students. Include the plan and any recommendations in the portfolio.

☐ c) With the permission of administration, participate in an interview for a professional position. A critique of the interviewing process will be written and included in the portfolio.

☐ d) Gather information from two or more administrators on relevant and legal questioning/assessment strategies used in interviewing. Compile a list of questions to be used in hiring faculty or staff and include in the portfolio.

☐ e) Meet with persons responsible for personnel and discuss the role their department takes in planning for professional development, e.g., experience of present staff, current evaluations, future needs, etc. Include findings and recommendations in the portfolio.

☐ f) Meet with administrators at the district/school level and gather information on staff turnover, i.e., percentage, numbers in differing positions, and reasons for leaving. Gather any additional information from exit interviews. Assess the turnover rate, actions taken to address concerns, and any additional recommendations for improvement. Include assessment and recommendations in the portfolio.

☐ g) Meet with administrators at the district/school level and gather information on placement and promotion policy and procedures. Discuss numbers of teachers teaching outside of their certification areas and the extent to which the district/school promotes and develops from within. Include a summary of the major goals, concerns, and recommendations in the portfolio.

☐ h) Go to the Learning Forward website (www.learningforward.org) and review the National Staff Development Standards. Determine the adherence to these standards in any of the reviews and actions in above activities undertaken. Provide findings and a brief reflection in the portfolio.

♦ Other related activities approved by your supervisor, and/or service activities to district/school assigned by the supervisor, and/or activities that are part of a larger project.

29. *Faculty and Staff Evaluation*

Place an "X" by the activity or activities below that are approved or required by your school and university supervisor as part of your intern plan. You must choose at least ONE activity in this area but a majority to all of the activities are recommended for maximum learning and experience.

☐ a) Interview two to three respected administrators experienced in conducting teacher and staff evaluations. Solicit key learnings, concerns, do's and don'ts, and recommendations for evaluating faculty and staff. Provide highlights from the interviews in the portfolio.

☐ b) Lead a discussion or survey a group of representative teachers concerning teacher evaluation. Solicit perspectives on the fairness, relevance, and validity of the evaluation instrument used and the process of gathering evaluative data, e.g., observations, student test scores, etc. Also solicit recommendations for improving the instrument and/or the process. Provide findings and recommendations in the portfolio.

☐ c) Lead a discussion or survey a group of representative staff members concerning staff evaluation. Solicit perspectives on the fairness, relevance, and validity of the evaluation instrument used and the process of gathering evaluative data, e.g., observations, teacher input, etc. Also solicit recommendations for improving the instrument and/or the process. Provide findings and recommendations in the portfolio.

☐ d) Interview a leader of the local or state teachers union or association concerning teacher evaluation. Solicit current issues, grievances, goals, and recommendations for improving teacher evaluation. Provide the findings in the portfolio.

> ♦ Other related activities approved by your supervisor, and/or service activities to district/school assigned by the supervisor, and/or activities that are part of a larger project.

Professional Standards for Educational Leaders 2015

Standard 7

Professional Community for Teachers and Staff
Effective educational leaders foster a professional community of teachers and other professional staff to promote each student's academic success and well-being.

Skill and Performance Areas for Meeting Standard 7
30) Issue and Conflict Resolution
31) Professional Learning Communities
32) Distributive Leadership

30. *Issue and Conflict Resolution*

Place an "X" by the activity or activities below that are approved or required by your school and university supervisor as part of your intern plan. You must choose at least ONE activity in this area but a majority to all of the activities are recommended for maximum learning and experience.

☐ a) Choose a current issue at your district/school. Find at least two persons on either side of the issue. Meet with the chosen persons in a group or individually to ascertain the goals for each side. Ensure each side understands the goals of the other side. Develop a list of concerns that each side believes about the opposing side. Devise a resolution that helps both sides achieve their goals and addresses all concerns. Meet with both sides to reach consensus on the new proposal or plan. Include the goals, list of concerns, and consensus on goals in the portfolio. Include any recommendations for the school/district concerning the issue. Note: Choose professional school-related issues versus very sensitive or personal issues.

  ♦ Other related activities approved by your supervisor, and/or service activities to district/school assigned by the supervisor, and/or activities that are part of a larger project.

31. *Professional Learning Communities*

Place an "X" by the activity or activities below that are approved or required by your school and university supervisor as part of your intern plan. You must choose at least ONE activity in this area but a majority to all of the activities are recommended for maximum learning and experience.

☐ a) Meet with a grade-level or department team and conduct a professional learning community (PLC) audit. Following an analysis of the findings, discuss the merits of PLCs, concerns, and recommendations to overcome any barriers to its implementation. Examples of audit questions:

- Are teachers observing each other's teaching?
- Is there time and support for this?
- Is there a culture of transparent practices being developed?
- Are teachers open to new learning, change?
- Does the principal facilitate and collaborate with faculty on learning?
- Are successful practices, learning from extended training, and/or instructional concerns shared between grade-level or department faculty?
- Does the shared vision of the school incorporate what's done for individual students not learning?
- Is learning assessed in a timely manner (weekly, every three or six weeks) and does it focus on individual students versus class or school averages?
- Has trust been developed among teachers and between faculty and administration?
- Do staff development opportunities support professional learning communities?

☐ b) Lead a grade-level, department, or entire faculty PLC activity. Have each teacher solicit from their students answers to the following six questions. Delete any responses that are very personal in nature and compile responses to each question. Present and discuss the findings.

1) What are the things I do that help you learn?
2) What things should I change or stop doing to better help you learn?
3) What additional things can I do to help you learn?
4) What are the things I do that help you enjoy our class?
5) What things should I change or stop doing to help you better enjoy our class?
6) What additional things can I do to help you enjoy our class?

Include findings and recommended actions in the portfolio.

- Other related activities approved by your supervisor, and/or service activities to district/school assigned by the supervisor, and/or activities that are part of a larger project.

32. *Distributive Leadership*

Place an "X" by the activity or activities below that are approved or required by your school and university supervisor as part of your intern plan. You must choose at least ONE activity in this area but a majority to all of the activities are recommended for maximum learning and experience.

☐ a) Attain permission from the principal to observe or, even better, participate in the Site-Based Decision-Making (SBDM) team. Document agenda, actions taken, and results. Provide a reflection on the processes used and any suggestions for improvement. Present your findings to the SBDM team for discussion. Include findings and recommendations in the portfolio.

☐ b) Meet with several representative members of the SBDM team and solicit their perspectives on the degree of leadership they provide. Do they feel empowered to make decisions; feel they are solely advisory; feel that they are simply carrying out a task for administration? Discuss your findings with the principal or administrative team and include in the portfolio.

☐ c) Meet with several department or grade-level chairs and compile a list of leadership responsibilities for the position. Solicit their perspective on the degree of autonomy they exercise and recommendations for increased leadership responsibilities and power. Discuss your findings with the principal or administrative team and include in the portfolio.

☐ d) Meet with an officer of the teachers association/union and solicit current areas of concern and/or goals concerning distributive leadership for teachers. Discuss your findings with the principal or administrative team. After hearing both sides of this issue, what recommendations for resolution would you make if you were the principal? Include your recommendations in the portfolio.

♦ Other related activities approved by your supervisor, and/or service activities to district/school assigned by the supervisor, and/or activities that are part of a larger project.

Standard 7

Professional Standards for Educational Leaders 2015

Standard 8

Meaningful Engagement of Families and Community

Effective educational leaders engage families and the community in meaningful, reciprocal, and mutually beneficial ways to promote each student's academic success and well-being.

Skill and Performance Areas for Meeting Standard 8

33) Community/Public Relations
34) Parent Involvement
35) Community/Business Involvement and Partnerships

33. Community/Public Relations

Place an "X" by the activity or activities below that are approved or required by your school and university supervisor as part of your intern plan. You must choose at least ONE activity in this area but a majority to all of the activities are recommended for maximum learning and experience.

☐ a) Interview one or more persons involved in district/school public relations. The interview should include strategies for effective communication to and from the community and the issue of community politics. A summary of the interview will be included in the portfolio.

☐ b) With the person from activity (a) or another in the department, assist in the preparation of a written communication to be sent out to the public. A copy of the communication will be included in the portfolio.

☐ c) Investigate through knowledgeable persons in the district to ascertain the most influential groups and individuals in the community. Using brief phone interviews, discuss their assessment of communication with the district/school, issues and concerns, and recommendations for improved relations. Include a summary and recommendations in the portfolio.

☐ d) Using the summary and recommendations for (c), meet with one board member or district/school administrator, and compare his or her perspective and plans for improved community relations. Include a summary and recommendations in the portfolio.

☐ e) Meet with a member of the local media to ascertain his or her perspective in gathering and reporting school/district information. Include the perspective and any recommendations for more positive media recognition in the portfolio.

  ♦ Other related activities approved by your supervisor, and/or service activities to district/school assigned by the supervisor, and/or activities that are part of a larger project.

34. *Parent Involvement*

Place an "X" by the activity or activities below that are approved or required by your school and university supervisor as part of your intern plan. You must choose at least ONE activity in this area but a majority to all of the activities are recommended for maximum learning and experience.

☐ a) Develop a general questionnaire addressing school policy, instruction, homework, activities, discipline, and parent involvement. Distribute the questionnaire to a group of representative parents. A summary of the findings concerning parent attitudes about school will be included in the portfolio.

☐ b) Examine the current policy and procedures for parent involvement in the school/district, in particular, a plan for involving hard-to-reach parents. A brief summary of the district's/school's initiatives in parent involvement will be included in the portfolio.

☐ c) Write a brief proposal for increasing or improving parent involvement and attitude toward the school. The proposal will be included in the portfolio.

☐ d) Observe a meeting of the Site-Based Council. Assess the role of parents in the process and provide any recommendations for increasing the effectiveness of their role. The agenda, outcomes of the meeting, and recommendations will be included in the portfolio.

♦ Other related activities approved by your supervisor, and/or service activities to district/school assigned by the supervisor, and/or activities that are part of a larger project.

35. *Community Resources*

Place an "X" by the activity or activities below that are approved or required by your school and university supervisor as part of your intern plan. You must choose at least ONE activity in this area but a majority to all of the activities are recommended for maximum learning and experience.

☐ a) Compile a list of social agencies that are available to help and support the students, faculty, and administration. The list of agencies and their major services provided will be included in the portfolio.

☐ b) Interview one social service worker (identified in activity a) who provides assistance to students or faculty. The interview will focus on the needs of the clients served and the worker's view of the role of the school in meeting these needs. A summary of the interview and recommendations for improvement will be included in the portfolio.

☐ c) Interview two community leaders that reside in the district/school attendance zone. Focus on their perceptions of the quality of education, concerns, and recommendations for the schools. A summary of the interview will be included in the portfolio.

☐ d) Gather information on the resources available to the schools from community and business. Analyze the extent of utilization, make recommendations for improved cooperation and mutual benefit, and include these in the portfolio.

♦ Other related activities approved by your supervisor, and/or service activities to district/school assigned by the supervisor, and/or activities that are part of a larger project.

Standard 8

Professional Standards for Educational Leaders 2015

Standard 9

Operations and Management

Effective educational leaders manage school operations and resources to promote each student's academic success and well-being.

Skill and Performance Areas for Meeting Standard 9

36) General Office Administration/Technology
37) School Operations/Policies
38) Facility and Maintenance Administration/Safety and Security
39) Student Transportation
40) Food Services
41) Supervision of the Budget

36. General Office Administration/Technology

Place an "X" by the activity or activities below that are approved or required by your school and university supervisor as part of your intern plan. You must choose at least ONE activity in this area but a majority to all of the activities are recommended for maximum learning and experience.

☐ a) Examine the International Society for Technology in Education (ISTE) Technology Standards for Administrators Systemic Improvement Standard. (http://www.iste.org/standards/ISTE-standards/standards-for-administrators) Assess the implementation of technology to improve the organization through the effective use of information and technology resources. Devise a plan for actions to better meet the standard and include in the portfolio.

☐ b) Review the job descriptions and evaluation forms for the key office personnel at the district/school (e.g., secretary, administrative assistant, attendance officer). Following this review, meet with these persons (individually or as a group) to discuss their major duties, technology skills and applications, concerns, and recommendations for the actual work required and its relation to the job description and evaluation form and include in the portfolio.

☐ c) Observe the office secretary for a period of time in order to assess the needs and demands of his/her position, including access and usage of technology resources. Following the observation, substitute for the administrative secretary in duties agreeable with the secretary and administration for a set period of time. Include a summary of the needs and demands of this position and recommendations for improvement in the portfolio.

☐ d) Observe the district technology administrator or campus technology coach to assess the essential functions of his/her position. Following the observation, include a summary of the needs and demands of the position in relation to the needs and demands of district technology needs. Report your findings and observations in the portfolio.

☐ e) Inventory the current administrative technology in use, which should include phone systems, copy machines, fax equipment, security systems, computers, printers, and any other form of technology used for administration of the district/school. Include the major uses and any major concerns with these forms of technology. Then, review the National Technology Plan essential areas (http://www.ed.gov/sites/default/files/netp2010.pdf) and the district/school technology plan. Assess how the current technologies align with the national/district/school goals for implementation. Make recommendations for improvement and include in the portfolio.

Standard 9

☐ f) Review the policy and budget for administrative technology. Develop a plan to fund and implement recommended technology upgrades and/or new emerging technologies to meet the needs of the administrative staff. Share the plan with the principal and include in the portfolio.

☐ g) Examine the district/school/classroom websites and district/school policies for updating and maintaining accurate content. Make recommendations for improvement to support ongoing school management and operations and include in the portfolio.

☐ h) Service learning is a strategy that integrates meaningful community service with instruction and reflection to enrich the learning experience, teach civic responsibility, and strengthen communities (http://www.uncfsu.edu/civic-engagement/service-learning/definition-of-service-learning). Choose one of the following topics: (1) "Establishing Partnerships to Cut Costs," (2) "Social Innovation," or (3) your own. Target constituencies that should be involved and develop a conference, summit, or roundtable to help participants elaborate a common understanding of service learning to support your school to create a sustainable, innovative, whole-school approach. Include in the portfolio your rationale, objectives, plan, and selected strategies.

☐ i) The Family Educational Rights and Privacy Act of 1974 (FERPA) is a federal law that establishes rules and regulations regarding access to and disclosure of student records. The act applies to all educational institutions that are recipients of federal funding (http://www2.ed.gov/policy/gen/guid/fpco/ferpa/index.html). Review how student records are managed and maintained at your school. Devise a plan for actions to strengthen compliance and communication related to FERPA issues and include in the portfolio.

   ♦ Other related activities approved by your supervisor, and/or service activities to district/school assigned by the supervisor, and/or activities that are part of a larger project.

37. *School Operations/Policies*

Place an "X" by the activity or activities below that are approved or required by your school and university supervisor as part of your intern plan. You must choose at least ONE activity in this area but a majority to all of the activities are recommended for maximum learning and experience.

☐ a) Review the policies for district/school operations. Evaluate the extent to which the district/school is in compliance with these policies. Make recommendations for increasing compliance with these policies. Include the evaluation and recommendations in the portfolio.

☐ b) Meet with the district/school attendance officer. Discuss the rules, procedures, and ramifications of attendance on law, finance, and general school/district operations. Include the highlights and/or summary of the meeting in the portfolio.

☐ c) Review the procedures for the district/school opening and closing of the school year. Observe or take an active part in these procedures. Critique the effectiveness and major concerns of these procedures. Include the critique in the portfolio.

☐ d) Review the district/school crisis/emergency plans. Include a brief outline of the essential steps school administrators must take and include in the portfolio.

♦ Other related activities approved by your supervisor, and/or service activities to district/school assigned by the supervisor, and/or activities that are part of a larger project.

Standard 9

38. Facility and Maintenance Administration/Safety and Security

Place an "X" by the activity or activities below that are approved or required by your school and university supervisor as part of your intern plan. You must choose at least ONE activity in this area but a majority to all of the activities are recommended for maximum learning and experience.

☐ a) Examine reports from current local health and fire inspections and any other required state or federal reporting data on maintenance of the facilities. Examine building work orders and work accomplished for the district/school. A summary of findings and recommendations will be completed and included in the portfolio.

☐ b) Meet with the Director of Maintenance and/or Head Custodian and review job responsibilities and schedules of staff. Shadow/observe one custodian and/or maintenance person for a period of time (one hour, more if possible). A brief report from the meeting and observation, including the needs, concerns, and overall assessment of work performed, will be included in the portfolio.

♦ Other related activities approved by your supervisor, and/or service activities to district/school assigned by the supervisor, and/or activities that are part of a larger project.

39. Student Transportation

Place an "X" by the activity or activities below that are approved or required by your school and university supervisor as part of your intern plan. You must choose at least ONE activity in this area but a majority to all of the activities are recommended for maximum learning and experience.

☐ a) Interview the Director of Transportation and discuss current issues and needs for transportation. This should include costs, maintenance, personnel issues, training and safety, and student problems. A brief summary of the needs and issues will be included in the portfolio.

☐ b) With the permission of the Director, observe one bus driver during either a morning or an afternoon bus route. A summary of observations and any recommendations will be included in the portfolio.

☐ c) Review the policies for student transportation. Evaluate the extent to which the district/school is in compliance. Be sure to consider home-to-school, school-to-home, and co-curricular procedures. Include a brief summary of the finding and recommendations in the portfolio.

☐ d) Review incident and discipline referrals occurring on the buses. Interview several students and bus drivers for concerns and recommendations for safer and more efficient bus service. Include a brief summary of the finding and recommendations in the portfolio.

♦ Other related activities approved by your supervisor, and/or service activities to district/school assigned by the supervisor, and/or activities that are part of a larger project.

40. Food Services

Place an "X" by the activity or activities below that are approved or required by your school and university supervisor as part of your intern plan. You must choose at least ONE activity in this area but a majority to all of the activities are recommended for maximum learning and experience.

☐ a) Interview the district/school food service manager and discuss the current requirements, concerns, and current issues of the program. A summary of findings from the interview will be included in the portfolio.

☐ b) Observe a food service worker in the preparation and delivery of either a breakfast or a lunch meal. A summary of the observation focusing on the needs, concerns, and overall assessment of work performed will be included in the portfolio.

   ♦   Other related activities approved by your supervisor, and/or service activities to district/school assigned by the supervisor, and/or activities that are part of a larger project.

41. *Supervision of the Budget*

Place an "X" by the activity or activities below that are approved or required by your school and university supervisor as part of your intern plan. You must choose at least ONE activity in this area but a majority to all of the activities are recommended for maximum learning and experience.

☐ a) Examine the school (or district) budget and the various accounts under the discretion and responsibility of the administrator of study. Analyze the extent to which funds are directly related to increasing learning. A brief analysis of the major functions, planning, reporting, and major concerns will be noted and included in the portfolio.

☐ b) Interview the administrator responsible for the district finance/budget office. The interview should focus on administrative responsibility, guidelines, training, and any other major needs or concerns that the office requires of the position of study. An overview of the interview will be included in the portfolio.

☐ c) Participate in the budget planning process for the district/school. An overview of the process and any recommendations will be included in the portfolio.

☐ d) Complete a requisition for a service or supply item from a budgeted account. A copy of the requisition and a brief description of the path it follows for approval to be included in the portfolio.

☐ e) Familiarize yourself with the Association of School Business Officials (ASBO) website (www.asbo.org) to determine national trends and issues. List trends and/or issues found and include in the portfolio.

   ♦ Other related activities approved by your supervisor, and/or service activities to district/school assigned by the supervisor, and/or activities that are part of a larger project.

Professional Standards for Educational Leaders 2015

Standard 10

School Improvement

Effective educational leaders act as agents of continuous improvement to promote each student's academic success and well-being.

Skill and Performance Areas for Meeting Standard 10

42) Change Process
43) Current Issues Affecting Teaching and Learning
44) Professional Affiliations and Resources
45) School Improvement Planning

42. *Change Process*

Place an "X" by the activity or activities below that are approved or required by your school and university supervisor as part of your intern plan. You must choose at least ONE activity in this area but a majority to all of the activities are recommended for maximum learning and experience.

☐ a) Review board policy regarding innovations and change in the district/ school. Select two to three readings from respected journals and discuss content with faculty and administration. Assess the degree to which change theory is used to facilitate innovation and changes in district/ school programs and operations. Write a reflective statement on the topic and include it in the portfolio.

☐ b) Meet with a current leader involved in implementing a district/school change. Find out why the change was made and what steps were taken to make the change. Following this, survey several persons affected by the change and assess the support or nonsupport for the change. Analyze both the stage the person is at and recommend a means for moving the person(s) to the next stage of change. Summarize and include in the portfolio.

☐ c) In your selected local project, devise a plan for any change affecting other individuals. Choose two of these individuals and discuss how they internalized or resisted the change. Include findings and recommendations with your project summary.

  ♦ Other related activities approved by your supervisor, and/or service activities to district/school assigned by the supervisor, and/or activities that are part of a larger project.

43. *Current Issues Affecting Teaching and Learning*

Place an "X" by the activity or activities below that are approved or required by your school and university supervisor as part of your intern plan. You must choose at least ONE activity in this area but a majority to all of the activities are recommended for maximum learning and experience.

☐ a) Compile a list of current issues that affect teaching and learning. Use research literature and perspectives from administrators, teachers, students, parents, and business and community leaders in compiling the list. Assess the degree of importance and urgency for each issue. Include your list and assessment with any recommendations in your portfolio.

   ♦ Other related activities approved by your supervisor, and/or service activities to district/school assigned by the supervisor, and/or activities that are part of a larger project.

44. *Professional Affiliations and Resources*

Place an "X" by the activity or activities below that are approved or required by your school and university supervisor as part of your intern plan. You must choose at least ONE activity in this area but a majority to all of the activities are recommended for maximum learning and experience.

☐ a) Contact several persons experienced in the position of study and compile a list of professional associations, service organizations, and local, state, and federal agencies that provide expertise and service to the position. The list of resources and their major area of service are to be included in the portfolio.

☐ b) Visit the website of either the NAESP or NASSP and your respective state affiliate and compile a list of all services and information available to the principal. Consider joining the relevant association (state and/or national) and begin reading periodicals and keeping up with the advances and concerns of principals across the state and/or nation. Summarize your findings and the relevance to the current needs of your school in the portfolio.

☐ c) Submit a brief professional development plan. Plans should include deficiencies as well as strengths cited in the internship in the various learning areas. The plan should also include ongoing development with membership and service to pertinent organizations cited in the above activity. The development plan is to be included in the portfolio.

   ♦ Other related activities approved by your supervisor, and/or service activities to district/school assigned by the supervisor, and/or activities that are part of a larger project.

45. *School Improvement Planning*

Place an "X" by the activity or activities below that are approved or required by your school and university supervisor as part of your intern plan. You must choose at least ONE activity in this area but a majority to all of the activities are recommended for maximum learning and experience.

☐ a) Obtain and review the School Improvement Plan (SIP). Discuss with the principal or chair of the SIP planning committee the process used to develop the plan. Note persons involved, timelines, data collection, evaluation criteria, and major goals and concerns addressed and include in the portfolio.

☐ b) Meet with a group of representative teachers and discuss the efforts taken to address the SIP. Note problems encountered and level of knowledge and interest in the SIP. Compile a list of recommendations to better sync the SIP with individual classroom duties and goals and include in the portfolio.

☐ c) With permission of the principal, serve on the SIP committee. Note participation levels, expertise, and level of agreement of the members. Evaluate the process used, make recommendations for improvement, and include in the portfolio.

☐ d) Lead or participate in the evaluation of a school program, e.g., reading, bilingual, music, athletics, etc. From the findings, develop an action plan for program improvement and include in the portfolio.

☐ e) Meet with a group of representative teachers and compile a list of recommendations for greater emphasis on formative versus summative teacher evaluation. Present the findings to faculty and administration. Include the list and recommendations in the portfolio.

♦ Other related activities approved by your supervisor, and/or service activities to district/school assigned by the supervisor, and/or activities that are part of a larger project.

2.2 Skill and Performance Activities: Beyond the Standards

The following skill and performance activities are inherent in the professional standards addressed in the previous section but bear separate investigation, reflection, and development. Most of the following cut across the professional standards to varying degrees and signify areas of knowledge, skill, and disposition on topics of great importance to education. Additional reading is included to frame and assist in the intern activities that follow each topic.

46. Social Justice

Leadership for social justice comes out of a long-held concern for the general principles of ethical practice in public administration (Barnard, 1938; Simon, 1947; Terry, 1993; Adams & Balfour, 1998, 2009; Gerzon, 2006; Adams, 2011; Svara, 2014). In recent years, scholars and activists have raised more specific concerns about the importance of class, race, and gender to understanding equity in schools and opportunities across groups of learners (Grant & Sleeter, 1986; Marshall, 1988; Weis, 1988; Brown, 2004, 2006; Darling-Hammond, 2007; Blackmore, 2009; Dantley & Tillman, 2010; Marshall & Oliva, 2010). These concerns include priorities placed on bilingual education, multicultural curricula, affirmative action, special education, and remedial education and issues related to culture, language, and diversity, as well as the connections among family, school, and community.

Historically, the schools have been seen as both a vehicle for advancing social mobility and as a gatekeeper, reproducing social inequality (Tyack, 1976, 1993; Deschenes, Cuban, & Tyack, 2001; Katz & Rose, 2013). Advocates for the poor, racial and ethnic minorities, and marginalized populations point to the greater challenges faced by some students compared with others, as well as patterns of societal and institutional discrimination which is retranslated into a schooling experience that advantages some students and disadvantages others. They point out that some parents bring valued social capital and purchasing power, which helps their children be successful in school; that predominantly White and more affluent school boards prioritize certain policies (e.g., zero tolerance policies, curriculum tracking), which result in disparate outcomes across groups of students; and that there exists a predominantly White and female teacher population and similarly lower percentages of school administrators of color with different expectations across class, ethnic, and gender lines (Marshall, 1988; Moses, 2002; Darling-Hammond, 2007; Marshall & Oliva, 2010).

The result is a twofold disadvantage for poor students and for students of color: 1) they do not see themselves well represented in the roles and leadership of schools, and 2) there is less familiarity and/or cultural competence among teachers and administrators working with subpopulations of students different from themselves. Regardless of cause, very different patterns of educational achievement and attainment across subgroups exist, and these gaps among have remained stable since the 1970s (Berliner, 2006, 2009). Student graduation and dropout rates, tracking in math classes, two- and four-year college application and participation patterns, truancy rates and attendance patterns, suspension and expulsion rates, and an opportunity for schooling in one's home language are all areas of concern for the developing school principal.

Others point to the many examples of children, who, in spite of obstacles, move through the system successfully, earn good grades at school, and navigate upward in social mobility. For proponents of this view of schooling, schools provide the skills and opportunities for children to move beyond the circumstances of birth and accomplish their goals/dreams (for example, see Baker, 2014). While both views contain important truths, there is considerable evidence that children enter schooling very differently from one another, and that schools retranslate advantage across class and ethnic lines. There is also considerable evidence that some communities are increasingly less willing to pay the full costs of educating children that don't necessarily look like them or share their historical experiences (Glass, 2008).

Another indication of the increasing importance for issues related to justice in schools and in the preparation of school principals is that the "American dream" of social and economic independence is becoming increasingly under challenge. For many, economic independence and full entry into the workplace has been delayed until one's 30s. At the same time, the gap between the rich and poor is increasing, with the gap between the upper and middle class greater today than in previous decades (Berliner & Glass, 2014). Still others argue that market-based educational reform and the view of school leaders as "entrepreneurs" have moved leadership into more of a "transactional" approach, whereby transactions are more important than building trust and "relationships" (Tschannen-Moran, 2002; Anyon, 2009). Anyon (2009) suggests that it is time for principals to move beyond a traditional concern for building caring communities and developing trust and instead work towards changing *the conditions that work against both trust and care in schools – poverty, inequity, and hierarchy*" (italics in original) (Anyon, p. 3). Gary Anderson (2009) introduces the idea of *advocacy leadership*, which requires school leaders to advocate for equity and opportunity for students, families, and communities. In Anderson's view, school leaders need to challenge the status quo, fight against unjust relationships, and raise consciousness about the greater challenges faced by some more than others.

> An advocacy leader believes in the basic principles of a high quality and equitable public education for all children, and is willing to take risks to make it happen. Advocacy leaders tend to be skilled at getting beneath high-sounding rhetoric to the devil in the details. They are skeptical by nature. They know the difference between the trappings of democracy and the real thing. They refuse to collude in so-called

collaborative teams or distributed leadership endeavors that are inauthentic. For instance, they know when a site-based leadership team is rigged against low-income parents. They know when parents of children with disabilities are being railroaded in IEP meetings by school professionals. They know the hard ball politics of influential parents and the ways they work the system to get privileges for their children at the expense of others. They are not seduced by business models yet they don't close off any avenue of new ideas. They are skeptical of the idea that we can avoid the difficult give-and-take of politics by replacing politics with market based choice policies.

(Anderson, 2009, p. 22, cited in Anyon, 2011)

Social Justice in the *Professional Standards*

The Professional Standards for Educational Leaders 2015 (National Policy Board for Educational Administration, 2015) continues the commitments to leadership and social justice that were identified in previous versions of national standards for educational leadership (Council of Chief State School Officers, 2008). The Standards explicitly references the term social justice in elaborating the work that is necessary to meet the standard (Standards 1 and 2):

Standard 1. Mission, Vision, and Core Values
Effective educational leaders develop, advocate, and enact a shared mission, vision, and core values of high-quality education and academic success and well-being of each student. Effective Leaders

c) Articulate, advocate, and cultivate core values that define the school's culture and stress the imperative of child-centered education; high expectations and student support; equity, inclusiveness, and social justice; openness, caring, and trust; and continuous improvement.

Standard 2. Ethics and Professional Norms
Effective educational leaders act ethically and according to professional norms to promote each student's academic success and well-being. Effective Leaders:

d) Safeguard and promote the values of democracy, individual freedom and responsibility, equity, social justice, community, and diversity.

(National Policy Board for Educational Administration, 2015)

Other standards explicitly commit to equity, diversity, care, community, and student well-being.

Standard 3. Equity and Cultural Responsiveness
Effective educational leaders strive for equity of educational opportunity and culturally responsive practices to promote *each* student's academic success and well-being.

Standard 5. Community of Care and Support for Students
Effective educational leaders cultivate an inclusive, caring, and supportive school community that promotes the academic success and well-being of *each* student.

Standard 6. Professional Capacity of School Personnel
Effective educational leaders develop the professional capacity and practice of school personnel to promote *each* student's academic success and well-being.

Standard 7. Professional Community for Teachers and Staff
Effective educational leaders foster a professional community of teachers and other professional staff to promote *each* student's academic success and well-being.

Standard 8. Meaningful Engagement of Families and Community
Effective educational leaders engage families and the community in meaningful, reciprocal, and mutually beneficial ways to promote *each* student's academic success and well-being.
(National Policy Board for Educational Administration, 2015)

We would argue that these commitments define school leaders to be not only aware of but also actively engaged in building a more just and equitable educational environment that serves the needs of all children and families. At the same time, the current educational reform priorities (e.g., raising student test scores, promoting high-stakes testing, adopting value-added methods of teacher and principal evaluation, and recognizing the contribution of school leadership on student learning outcomes) place additional pressures on school principals to meet these accountability demands. How you, as a school leader, learn to balance competing priorities *and* be an advocate for justice is an important part of the learning that comes from your internship experience.

Social Justice in the Internship
One of the concerns of those charged with developing graduate degree programs in educational leadership and in the internship experiences is that press of everyday events will swamp a novice practitioner's capacity to consider these broader conditions that surround education and schooling. While some of you may think these concerns are outside the purview of school administrators, we would argue that mastering the specifics of one's job and doing the right thing should not be considered separately. The press of daily events and conflicts that are an inevitable part of school environments should not prevent a novice from learning not only what to do to keep their job, but also an appreciation of what it means to do the job "right." Vickers

(1995) calls this heightened understanding the "appreciative system," and others (Cooperrider & Srivasrtva, 1987; Cooperrider & Whitney, 2005) have suggested the need for a more "appreciative inquiry" in the education of leaders, which includes a more interconnected (systems) approach to leadership and schooling that takes into account the many factors within and outside of one's school and district.

In courses taken during your leadership program or development, the limits of viewing the school principal as simply a manager are likely covered (De Pree, 1989, 1993; Bennis, 2003; Senge, 2009). Other models consider the school leader as designer or architect (Senge, 1990), instructional leader (Murphy, 2002), mediator (Gerzon, 2006), or advocate (Anderson, 2009). Again, school administrators need to be not only attentive to the local culture in one's school/district, but also familiar with the larger picture of what happens to the students at home and in the community. Part of your emerging competence as a school leader will come from a deeper understanding of the research and appreciation of the data/resources that provide a more complete picture of school and community than is available by looking only at student test score outcomes.

Attending to Justice Issues in Your Internship

The view presented in this text is that the internship is a multifaceted learning process in which candidates integrate theory with practice by learning and practicing the craft of educational leadership. Through a series of leadership development experiences in an apprenticeship-like process, candidates develop leadership skills and a career orientation, assess their commitment to a career in the field, and receive feedback on their developing leadership skills and performance.

Issues related to justice are important; it is our view that your responses to these new understandings will ultimately be one of the milestones for determining your success as a school administrator.

We also live in an age of "big data." Accountability and assessment data are all around you, and during your internship experience you will need to inform yourself about what data exist and how data can help you to understand your school population and patterns of student success and failure. For example, have you considered:

- Preschool participation and subsequent elementary school achievement?
- 4th-grade reading level and its relationship to subsequent dropout or success?
- Social-emotional learning and its relationship to grades and learning outcomes?
- Challenges related to transition points – elementary to middle school, middle to high school? Who benefits and who is disadvantaged in current policies and practices?

Table 2 Social Justice Leadership Framework

Recognition	Reversal	Redistribution
Awareness of *self* as separate from cultural, historical context. Awareness of culture and history as factors in disparate educational outcomes.	Awareness of *self* in context, culture, history, and acceptance as a benefactor of disparate educational outcomes.	Awareness of *self* in context of own power and privilege and acceptance of role in eradicating inequitable systems.
Develop self-consciousness.	Develop critical thinking and an equity conscious. Develop analytic skills to identify inequities in opportunities and outcomes.	Develop critical interculturalism (locally/globally). Develop action-oriented skills to challenge and dismantle systems of inequity.
Tolerate individual differences as necessary.	Appreciate and accommodate group differences.	Value difference as a source of organizational/systemic strength and learning.
Focus on racism of *others*.	Focus on *individual* "-isms."	Focus on *institutional* "-isms."
Localize effort in a personal context.	Localize effort in local/national context.	Localize effort in global/transnational context that recognizes human and ecological connectivity.
Develop an awareness of the capacity of leadership to foster social justice.	Develop capacity to facilitate resources, programs, and policy equity to reverse inequitable outcomes and counter marginalizing forces. Recognize barriers to student progress and create reactive systems and structures. Develop the capacity to be a change agent to facilitate social justice. Develop capacity to advocate for individuals/groups who suffer marginalization. Enhance capacity to work on microsystem equity to address and/or compensate inequities.	Extend capacity to work on macrosystem equity and transformation to prevent future inequities. Develop capacity to facilitate resource, programs, and policy equity to redistribute access, opportunities, and conditions. Develop capacity to create intercultural organization and proactive systems. Make unequal distribution of resources to eradicate unequal conditions.
Maintain power in order to address needs of other.	Share power in order to empower others.	Relinquish power in order to allow others to empower themselves.

- ♦ Differential discipline/suspension/expulsion rates and alternatives that may limit disparate outcomes?
- ♦ Patterns of dropouts and school leavers in your school and community?
- ♦ School to prison pipeline in your school and district?
- ♦ Opportunities for participatory planning and budgeting, which build greater participation among school and community members?

Attending to local practices related to equity, fairness, and justice during your principal internship means learning to do the right thing in the face of competing pressures. Building structures that include the collaboration and participation of various partners is a first step. Good principals recognize that while individual people have a stake in what happens to a particular child at school, there is also a public good in understanding how education and schooling contribute to a more democratic and just society for all.

What Can You Do?

Some schools, districts, and even states have recently passed legislation or policy that opens up opportunities for new projects related to equity and accountability. In California, for example, a new school funding formula (Local Control Funding Formula – LCFF) passed in 2012 requires school districts to engage local stakeholders in the budget process. One approach to build meaningful engagement in schools has been participatory budgeting (PB), a democratic process in which school and community members directly decide how to spend a portion of a public budget. With support from Californians for Justice, one San Jose school district held a town hall meeting in which over 150 students, parents, teachers, and administrators participated. The meeting highlighted participatory budgeting as a way to brainstorm and prioritize spending to support the needs of low-income students and families. Participants divided into multiple groups to explore and focus on spending priorities to address different issues including school climate, college access, and parent engagement. School board members met with high school freshmen, parents met with teachers, students talked with each, all to create and concrete proposals to spend funds to address their needs. The pilot project led to an actual PB event in which students voted on how best to spend $50,000 of the school's discretionary funding.

> After a months-long campaign and a week of voting, students put themselves literally in the driver's seat. They voted to spend the money on trips for 50 students to tour Southern California colleges, new uniforms for sports teams, and, in first place, a six-hour driver education course for at least 30 students. The $9,600 expenditure will reinstate a driver education program that the East Side Union High School District once offered. Its elimination created a financial hardship for the school's primarily low-income families, which have had to pay the approximately $300 in costs for a six-hour driving course plus a $30 fee for a written test, students said.
>
> (Fensterwald, 2015)

This illustration on participatory budgeting and the concerns raised in this section are part of the concerns and responsibilities of school leaders. You are urged to consider leadership as a larger calling that is connected to justice and learn to embrace new competencies in your repertoire. The words are easy; the job of doing something, of building opportunities and structures that nourish the public good, is hard.

Social Justice Activities

Place an "X" by the activity or activities below that are approved or required by your school and university supervisor as part of your intern plan. You must choose at least ONE activity in this area but a majority to all of the activities are recommended for maximum learning and experience.

a) Evaluate a school policy that may intentionally or unintentionally limit educational opportunities for some students. Review how other similar districts address the same policy dilemma and interview school or district officials about how alternative policy approaches might achieve more equitable, fair outcomes. Propose new policies.

b) Engage in advocacy with the local school leadership team or school board about changing a school policy or practice to reduce bias and improve fairness for all students, while supporting improved student learning.

c) Evaluate current district and state education policies for their social justice implications. Track the history and current state of these policies and the equity concerns they raise (such as related to school funding, charter schools, and school desegregation). Evaluate the current equity consequences of these policies for your school. Write a memo to your school principal about the policy and its consequences, proposing alternatives.

♦ Other related activities approved by your supervisor, and/or service activities to district/school assigned by the supervisor, and/or activities that are part of a larger project.

47. Action Research

The job of school principal may be one of the toughest jobs in the nation. Numerous studies have shown the impact of school leadership on student achievement (Branch, Hanushek, & Rivkin, 2013). Educational leadership internship programs are responsible for preparing aspiring principals for the responsibilities and duties of the principalship. The quality of training principals receive in teacher preparation programs before they assume their positions has a lot to do with whether school leaders can meet the expectations of these jobs. Darling-Hammond, LaPointe, Meyerson, Orr, and Cohen (2007) and Gray (2007) found that the strong principal preparation programs provided their interns with practical experiences under the guidance of a skilled professional practitioner (mentor) supporting the development and understanding of critical leadership skills. Completing an action research project is one example of a practical field experience that prepares interns to initiate and facilitate inquiry into ongoing school improvement, as well as develop critical leadership skills.

Action research is a tool for continual research-based inquiry conducted to inform and improve student learning through a school improvement process. Action research allows students to explore the empirical realities of their campus and to reflect on these realities in light of current trends in the field and exemplary practices reported in the literature (Sappington, Baker, Gardner, & Pacha, 2010). Inquiry through action research follows a process that informs and guides change for improvement of student learning (Logan, 2014).

Research stresses the importance of a quality internship experience that involves extended opportunities to practice and apply learning (Gray, 2007; Browne-Ferrigno, 2011). Furthermore, Orr (2006) found that case- and problem-based teaching methods provide a deeper understanding of the role of leadership, not just as an instrument for school improvement, but also as a means of promoting social justice and democracy in our schools. According to Holter, Frabutt, and Nuzzi (2014), exemplary school leadership programs integrate instructional theory and practice to create active, field-connected learning, such as action research projects.

Leading an action research project allows interns to practice specific skills critical to effective educational leadership (Terry, 2010; Sappington et al., 2010; Osterman, Furman, & Sernak, 2014). When interns experience empowerment through collaboration with school stakeholders, they begin to realize their potential for leading inquiry and change. Beyond framing questions to investigate problems of practice, interns learn appropriate methods for collecting and analyzing data, as well as how to facilitate diverse stakeholder input. Additionally, interns create school climates that support student learning, advance a social justice agenda (Osterman et al., 2014), and develop communication and written skills.

Preparing Effective School Leaders
The role of the principal is complex and requires a broad range of knowledge and skills. According to Darling-Hammond et al. (2007), the quality education that aspiring principals receive in their preparation programs and a sustained effort on continuous growth after they are hired is a factor in whether or not they can meet the high expectations for the position.

Educator preparation programs should be delivered to best meet the needs of adult learners and to allow administrative interns to apply their learning in authentic settings with a focus on real-world problems and dilemmas (Davis, Darling-Hammond, LaPointe, & Meyerson, 2005). This can be accomplished with internships/practicums that require the application of acquired skills, knowledge, and problem-solving strategies within school settings. Kolb, Boyatzis, and Mainemelis (2001) found that real world practice increased a leader's ability to think about, examine, and systematically plan strategies for school improvement. Ideally, strong educator preparation programs provide interns with an intense internship/practicum that gives them opportunities to be a part of the day-to-day operations of the school environment under the supervision of an expert mentor. In addition, educator preparation programs should provide the intern ample time to reflect on the activities and how those activities informed their future role as an administrator.

In order for the internship/practicum experience to aid in the development of effective school leaders, the field-based experiences need to be more than simplistic activities such as bus duties and observing campus/district meetings. The activities should give interns opportunities to demonstrate that they have the knowledge and skills to manage organizational change, create significant learning environments, lead a school-improvement initiative, communicate and work collaboratively with all stakeholders, and build capacity within the organization. To develop the knowledge and skills to successfully demonstrate the intern's proficiencies, a mentor principal is critical for providing guidance to interns.

Gray (2007) noted that good mentors are the key component of educator preparation programs designed to equip interns for continuous school improvement. Good mentorship for school leadership includes establishing a mindset for action research. Specifically, mentorship in action research can expand perspective, facilitate critical dialogue, and increase awareness with respect to practical, political, and justice issues that might be otherwise unnoticed. Therefore, mentors must be knowledgeable toward purposeful research and provide quality feedback at each stage of the action research cycle (Wright, 2014), from (a) identifying a problem, (b) gathering data, (c) analyzing and interpreting data, (d) formulating an action plan, (e) implementing the plan, (e) evaluating the outcomes, (f) amending the plan, and (g) taking a second action step.

This collaborative work also sets apart the school leader from the classroom teacher. Internship/practicum activities should be structured for solving school issues – the heart of action research. At first, opportunities might be observing and participating as part of an action research team, shifting to a leadership role for identifying and implementing school improvement interventions. As noted by Frels, Newman, and Newman (2015), research mentoring provides a platform for dialogue, introspection of personal qualities, critical thinking, patience with the research process, and self-directed lifelong learning. By infusing action research in the internship/practicum experience, real school problems become opportunities for leadership to transform interns before they leave the starting gate for their first principalship.

Action Research and Continuous School Improvement

Schools are buffeted by expectations and demands from many sources: local, state, and national, as well as global. These expectations come in the guise of local mandates or state and national laws outlining performance goals for students and teachers; they are further impacted by our real-time connections to 21st-century global issues and economies. Within this maelstrom of competing demands, educational leaders are tasked with navigating these ever-changing currents to ensure that all students emerge from their preK–12 learning experiences ready to leverage available career and post-secondary opportunities. The urge to reach for a superhero cape is almost irresistible.

Educational leaders have a multitude of resources for addressing issues and concerns on their campus. Research, specifically action research, can be used as a component of the broader campus vision and strategic planning process contributing to school renewal and instructional improvement (Glanz, 2014). Moreover, action research allows school leaders, existing and aspiring, to identify and study in real time simple as well as more complex school issues that are not easily answered. These issues that seem to appear on a daily basis become more fully understood and addressed when viewed through the lens of action research (Johnson, Smith, Willis, Levine, & Haywood, 2011; Glanz, 2014). Further, Koshy (2005) suggested action research supports the reflection and evaluation processes inherent to making needed changes in school practices.

Interns in educational leadership preparation programs have indicated that solving concerns on their campus through the process of action research allowed them to practice the leadership tasks that would be integral to their future leadership roles (Sappington et al., 2010). Aspiring leaders also developed capacity for problem solving and leadership decision-making through tackling concerns dealing with ethics, justice, equity, and authentic learning (Batagiannis, 2011). Leadership interns further suggested that participating in action research on their campus helped them in the following ways: a) transforming their thinking and practices; b) learning to lead through more inclusive and democratic processes; and c) recognizing that the action research process supported improvement of school processes and climate (Wood & Govender, 2013).

Action Research and Social Justice

At the crux of action research are the social issues that surround it, including the inequalities in educational practices that influence the status quo. Before embarking on educational action research, it is important to examine your own position as a researcher with respect to your worldview, belief systems, values, and influences and biases that impact research. Especially important for action researchers is the goal to provide background – which becomes part of the conceptual framework in the research design. The philosophical stances help to position ideas with respect to how and why the research questions were formed, what data are to be collected and interpreted, and how subsequent interventions and actions were created for the action cycle.

As noted by Mills (2014), the self-reflection process in action research is a rich opportunity for clarifying how theoretical and worldview beliefs are interwoven through decisions for social changes by contextualizing data and outcomes. As you reflect, it is important to articulate and document how your ideas align with tenets of social justice and attend to any gaps in resources, access, or opportunities for underserved populations. Worldview beliefs help to provide context for data because they expose researcher mindset, overarching philosophy of life, values, outlook on life, formula for life, ideology, or even faith. Without doubt, a worldview influences the overall lens for seeing and interpreting all of the action research cycle. Actually, worldview even influences how and why the research questions were formed and the way in which a researcher believes that knowledge, or reality, is explored. Therefore, finding the balance between worldview and philosophical stance becomes a thread throughout each decision in action research and provides a needed context and rationale(s) for stakeholders and other interested persons.

Charmaz (2005) contended that a critical lens in research helps to examine what people say and compare it to what they do for attending to contradictions between myths and realities, rhetoric and practice, and ends and means. She emphasized that a social justice focus allows the researcher to recognize how resources, hierarchies, access, and disabling conditions are interrelated to power and subsequent practices. The following three areas help to highlight some advocacy considerations to integrate social justice as a research lens (or philosophical stance):

1) **Resources:** Who controls the resources? Who needs them? How, if at all, are resources shared, concealed, or distributed? How did the current situation arise?
2) **Social Hierarchies:** What are they? What actual purposes do these hierarchies serve? Who benefits from them? How, if at all, do definitions of race, class, gender, and age cluster in specific hierarchies? Which moral justifications support the observed hierarchies? Who promulgates these justifications and how do they circulate?
3) **Consequences of Social Policies and Practices:** What are some rules – both tacit and explicit? Who writes or enforces them? Whose interests do the rules reflect? Do the rules and routine practices negatively affect certain groups or categories of individual?

Through each step of the action research process, the use of philosophical guiding questions helps to integrate the philosophical lens. In short, the philosophical stance frames the *what* and the *why* of the research process. Most importantly, establishing and documenting your philosophical stance provides the important rigor for molding your identity as a researcher and for building sound future research practices in your field and community.

Action Research Process

The action research process is grounded in collaborative problem solving supported by collegiality and mutual learning (Batagiannis, 2011; Osterman et al., 2014). Further, working in a collaborative leadership role with colleagues enables implementation of action research on a larger scale. Reflection is integral to the action research process and is applied by researchers before, during, and after the implementation of action research (Johnson et al., 2011). In conducting action research, school leaders engage in a cycle of assessing areas of performance to identify issues or problems, review relevant research about their topic, develop interventions to impact areas of concern, monitor progress and performance through data collection and analysis, learn from the results of the study, and reflect on next steps in the process (Sagor, 2009). Applying the systemic process of the action research cycle allows for ongoing problem solving specific to the needs of individual campuses, supports a continuous improvement process, and provides the intern the "opportunity to rehearse the leadership tasks they will face in coming years" (Sappington et al., 2010, pp. 266–267).

An important aspect of leadership is the ability to communicate effectively and share knowledge. The final steps in the action research process are writing a formal organized report (Mills, 2014) and sharing your research with others (Dana, 2009). An action research report is usually written using an academic writing style and format. The report is presented in a logical, orderly manner so that it is easily understood by the reader.

The following are common sections of an action research report. However, there are multiple ways that an action research report may be organized. Most colleges and universities have developed their own required format and style. Check with your instructor about the style and format used in your institution.

- ◆ Title Page
- ◆ Abstract – An overall summary of the completed action research study.
- ◆ Introduction – Includes the introduction, background, problem statement/research question(s), and significance of the study.
- ◆ Review of the Literature – Review of related literature from experts in the field organized by subheadings.
- ◆ Research Design – Discussion of participants, procedures, data collection, and analysis.
- ◆ Findings – In this section, discuss the results from data analysis.
- ◆ Conclusions and Recommendations – This section begins with a brief summary of the project, then a discussion of the conclusion that can be drawn from the findings, followed by a reflection on the entire study, then a discussion of recommendations based on findings and closing concluding remarks.
- ◆ References – Provide the context for your report.

Writing your report is not the last step of your action research. Publicly sharing your research with stakeholders on your campus and others will complete the action research process (Dana, 2009) . . . until your next wondering sets you off on another journey of inquiry.

Action Research Activity

a) The intern will design, lead, collect, and analyze data and communicate findings and implications for further action steps in a formal action research study to address an identified need on their campus. It is highly recommended that the intern lead a group of teachers in the study. The group should find consensus on the cause of the problem to be addressed, intervention, timeline, and type of data to collect. Following consensus on these, the intern should meet with the principal to discuss the study and gain approval.

48. Dispositions and Interpersonal Skills

A critical part of each candidate's fieldwork is the development of effective dispositions and interpersonal skills. According to the Merriam-Webster online dictionary, a disposition is "a tendency to think or act in a particular way." Leadership experts agree that selected dispositions are critical for effective leadership practice, and that leadership knowledge and skills are insufficient without these (Bryk, Sebring, Allensworth, Luppescu, & Easton, 2010; Louis, Leithwood, Wahlstrom, & Anderson, 2010). Hackett and Hortman (2008) argue that dispositions "motivate the application of knowledge and skills." In recent years, a variety of dispositions have been highlighted as critical for effective leadership practice, particularly those related to ethics, caring, social justice, and change-oriented dispositions (Brown, 2006; Gerstl-Pepin, Killeen, & Hasazi, 2006; Wagner et al., 2006; Theoharis, 2007). More recently, there has been attention to emotional intelligence (Goleman, 1998) and the emotional competencies that are positively associated with leadership and organizational outcomes.

Yet, developing dispositions for educational leaders can be challenging (Tishman, Jay, & Perkins, 1993). Several leadership preparation programs have adopted an experiential and reflective learning approach to developing leadership candidates' dispositions, organized around those most essential to effective leadership practices (Creasap, Peters, & Uline, 2005; McKenzie, Skrla, & Scheurich, 2006; Rucinski & Bauch, 2006). Thus, there appears to be conditions under which leadership dispositions can be developed – when they can be defined and assessed to set learning goals and measure progress and when interns use reflective practices to question existing assumptions and consider and try out alternatives (Osterman & Kottkamp, 2004; Creasap et al., 2005).

According to Osterman and Kottkamp (2004), reflective practice is an effective means of experiential learning for leadership development. It enables leadership candidates to develop an awareness of their habitual actions and assumptions and consider their effectiveness relative to intentions. Learning through reflective practice is guided by Kolb's four learning stages – having (1) concrete experiences; (2) analyzing and questioning one's assumptions and actions in these experiences; (3) considering alternatives through reconceptualization; and (4) active experimentation with new actions and approaches (Kolb, 1984). This cycle can be formalized in a learning plan to guide candidates' learning. Drawing from their own experiences and a program's priority dispositions, candidates can analyze and reflect upon his or her dispositions – both actions and assumptions – and consider alternative approaches.

Once identified, a candidate can create a disposition-related learning plan on what the learning activities he or she might use to try out new actions and assumptions. Specific, focused assignments can enable candidates to develop specific dispositions. Structuring learning experiences as part of the active experimentation phase can promote learning. Brown, for example, found that by participating in assignments requiring the examination of assumptions, values and beliefs, and competing worldviews, leadership candidates can transform their dispositions around social justice and equity (Brown, 2006).

Below are some common dispositions and interpersonal skills that can be constructively developed through advisement and internship supervision. Candidates and advisors identify one or more dispositions and interpersonal skills to be a focus each semester and select ways that this skill or disposition can be developed and progress assessed. As appropriate, these and others may be discussed with the internship supervisor.

- Timeliness (such as completing tasks and paperwork on time).
- Thoroughness (such as doing more than is minimally required).
- Initiative (such as speaking up, suggesting activities or solutions, and taking advantage of opportunities).
- Encouragement of others (such as creating opportunities for others to participate in group discussions or tasks, encouraging others to speak up, and actively listening).
- Perspective taking (such as being able to respectfully consider others' points of view and constructively question one's own point of view).
- Organizational ability (such as being able to create systems and routines for tasks and responsibilities and to prioritize what needs to be done).
- Open and enabling orientation to problems and solutions (such as adapting educational experiences for all children, trying out ideas suggested by other staff members).

- ◆ Flexibility and willingness to be innovative (adapting easily to changing conditions, seeing opportunities for improved practice in new reforms, trying out ways to improve practice).
- ◆ Willingness to question constructively (being able to raise questions and make suggestions that are constructive and enable problem solving).

Candidates begin with a self-assessment to select a disposition or inter-personal skill to strengthen or improve. They then discuss their selection with the advisor for feedback and strategy. The candidate and advisor decide on a relevant short-term goal, the evidence of progress toward it, and strategies for skill acquisition and mastery through the internship or other experiences. Finally, the candidate and advisor decide how progress is to be documented and how to use journal reflections to support skill/disposition development over the internship.

For example, using this approach, one intern wanted to improve her ability to speak up and take initiative in small group committee meetings. She measured her frequency as a baseline and set a personal goal to increase the frequency of her initiative taking and contributing in group discussions. She informed her committee colleagues about her goal and solicited their feedback on her progress, as well as logged her own efforts. Over time, she increased the frequency and at the same time became more comfortable with taking initiative and actively contributing in small group meetings.

Disposition and Interpersonal Skill Activity

a) Describe the personal leadership dispositions and interpersonal skills (e.g., perspective taking, initiative, and timeliness) that will be developed during the internship. Follow the steps below for each disposition and skill chosen.
   1) Clarify the target disposition and/or interpersonal skill.
   2) Brainstorm possible activities to address the target disposition or skill as a means of improvement.
   3) Identify reflection strategies.
   4) Brainstorm possible indicators and means of assessment.
   5) Evaluate the plan for feasibility and potential success (Too much? Too little? Likely to lead to success?).

Prioritize the list from above and choose one or two of highest importance upon which to begin a focus. Initiate activities and after meeting your goal for the disposition or skill, begin a focus and activities on the next highest one on your list. Continue until you have met all of your goals.

49. New Technologies

Technology can no longer be viewed as a tool you just "add" to the learning environment; it has become ubiquitous and has grown to the point where it must be considered as an extension of human performance capabilities, having a utilitarian function in the same way we view electricity as a utility that powers our lives. People today do not think about electricity turning on their lights; it is just there, it works, and it is simply part of their living environment. Likewise, leaders need to view and use technology in the same way as a foundational element of the learning environment. This view enables us to build on the priorities of STEM (science, technology, engineering, and math) and incorporates the creativity of STEAM (science, technology, engineering, arts, and math), which is crucial to solving challenges learners face in the 21st century (Johnson, Adams Becker, Estrada, & Freeman, 2015).

In addition, this shift in thinking is necessary to reinvent how current traditional schools operate. It is more important than ever before for prospective school administrators to explore creative and innovative ways to use technology to remove limitations within the learning environment. This shift in thinking is also necessary to match the way learners view the world, as today's students are digital natives (Prensky, 2001). Since birth, various forms of technology have been an integral part of their lives and they expect regular technology accessibility during instruction. School leaders need to be aware of the ways technology can effectively contribute to higher student achievement and support continued school improvement initiatives.

School administrators need to become familiar with the ways emerging technologies can facilitate efficiency, collaboration, and personalization for learning and communication. Using a variety of cloud-based resources, mobile devices, and online learning communities promotes a green learning environment and reduces time and funds needed to maintain traditional systems. Furthermore, interns need to learn about the ethical and social aspects of technology use. This includes familiarization with district and federal policies related to the use of various forms of technologies by minors and staff, such as the Internet, databases, file sharing, and email.

Technology Today and Tomorrow

Many digital resources for teaching and learning in today's schools are free and easily obtained. Virtual worlds, online learning, and Web 2.0 tools invade our world (Lemke & Coughlin, 2009). Thousands of education apps cover everything from math and science to foreign languages and reading. Students can use a variety of mobile devices to manipulate math equations using just a finger, browse an interactive periodic table of elements, or engage in collaboration with their peers or the teacher. School administrators must take the lead in using technology to enhance learning. Building a vision for using new tools to support educational change is the responsibility of all school administrators. Research shows that students who use technology tools every day achieve at higher levels. Learning to use the latest digital tools empowers the campus and the district leader to assist others in understanding the need and support for an all-the-time-and-everywhere learning environment.

Technology today is more than word processing and spreadsheets of the past, although those productivity tools continue to be important. As predicted by Solomon and Schrum (2010), Web 2.0 resources and beyond are reaching a critical mass and the tools are easier to use, more transparent, and a necessary part of work at school. Cloud computing is a recognized resource on most campuses today. Working in the cloud simply means that information is stored on the Internet and can be attained and used by the owner from anywhere. The information no longer resides only on the personal computer at home or in school. This shift in focus of technology as a utility means shared resources, software, and information on demand can enable higher levels of student creativity and deeper learning.

Students can now create and submit learner-centered reflective portfolios digitally as ePortfolios. When outside of school, students text, use instant messaging, and share Instagrams all while listening to music and browsing the Web. The Kaiser Family Foundation Report 7593 (as cited by Lemke & Coughlin, 2009) reveals that despite being heavy users of technology: "Most students do not know how to use the tools instructionally to become intelligent learners, creative producers, and effective communicators." We are responsible for modeling and using these tools to teach the children how to become informed communicators and consumers.

Students and teachers should focus on finding, synthesizing, and analyzing information, then using it to create knowledge collaboratively and communicating the results – all online, as we move to Web-based operations in the cloud. Solomon and Schrum (2010) also predict that district operations will move to the cloud.

In addition to this move to the cloud, the annual Horizon Report (Johnson et al., 2015) points to the following major trends:

- ◆ Increased use of blended learning
- ◆ Rise of STEAM learning
- ◆ Increased use of collaborative learning
- ◆ Shift from students as consumers to creators
- ◆ Rethinking of how schools work
- ◆ Shift to deeper learning approaches.

(Read the report at http://www.nmc.org/publication/nmc-horizon-report-2015-k-12-edition/)

What Do Prospective School Administrators Need to Know About Technology?

It may be the first time in our public school experience where many students are more knowledgeable and proficient in consumer technology than their teachers. This condition gives rise to the concept, promoted over many years, of including student input in the choice of learning activities and modalities. In short, educators can try to compete with tech-savvy students or utilize their knowledge and skill for school improvement. Regardless of advances in technology, it is part of our world and new school leaders should:

- Keep abreast of emerging technologies and their impact on school improvement.
- Utilize school, district, and grant resources to maintain updated technology resources. Elicit assistance from school community stakeholders.
- Become very familiar with the ethical and social aspects of technology usage. This component includes a full understanding of district and federal policies related to the use and abuse of various forms of technologies by minors and staff such as the Internet, databases, file sharing, email, and digital archiving.
- Understand that technologies should be interoperable rather than working in isolation. Shift your personal and organizational cultural thinking toward technology as a utility that becomes a foundational part of the learning environment.
- Provide ongoing support and resources for faculty and staff professional development related to technology applications and integration into the curriculum.
- Recognize online learning has become a critical resource and learning medium for all ages.
- Participate in Online Professional Learning Communities and develop a Personalized Learning Plan.

Clark's idea that technology should be used to enhance instruction, not replace good instruction, is important as we work to provide the best educational experiences for our students. He stated that "The best current evidence is that media are mere vehicles that deliver instruction but do not influence student achievement any more than the truck that delivers our groceries causes changes in our nutrition" (Clark, 2012, p. 2). Technology simply helps us become better instructors in addressing our learners' needs.

New Technologies Activities

Place an "X" by the activity or activities below that are approved or required by your school and university supervisor as part of your intern plan. You must choose at least ONE activity in this area but a majority to all of the activities are recommended for maximum learning and experience.

a) Develop a systematic process for implementing new technologies. Determine how to provide professional development and training for teachers prior to implementation. Determine how to evaluate and develop instructional support for implementing technology. Describe the process used, discuss concerns, and make any recommendations for improvement.

b) Your school has received monies for technology, and you have been chosen to search, evaluate, purchase, and implement the use of new software applications including simulation, visualization, and learning authoring tools such as LMS, Captivate, Powerpoint, etc. Collect information about two of the applications and develop a tool comparing application features, advantages, and disadvantages. Next, make recommendations to the board for purchase. Include in the portfolio your report and a plan for training and implementing use of these technologies.

c) Review the International Society for Technology in Education (ISTE) Technology Standards for Administrators to effectively leverage technology for learning: (http://www.iste.org/standards/ISTE-standards/standards-for-administrators). Create a plan to implement two or three of the five standards. Consider the essential conditions as you create your plan (http://www.iste.org/standards/essential-conditions). Share the plan in a blog and solicit input from colleagues for improvement. Summarize your findings and include in the portfolio.

d) Review the International Society for Technology in Education (ISTE) for Teachers (http://www.iste.org/standards/ISTE-standards/standards-for-teachers). Consider the essential conditions as you create your plan (http://www.iste.org/standards/essential-conditions). Research ways the school administration could support improving teacher technology proficiencies and technology implementation for instruction. Include your recommendations in the portfolio.

e) Examine the International Society for Technology in Education (ISTE) for Students (http://www.iste.org/standards/ISTE-standards/standards-for-students). Consider the essential conditions as you create your plan (http://www.iste.org/standards/essential-conditions). Write a plan about how you will support the implementation of a couple of technology standards for students for instruction. Include your plan in the portfolio.

50. School Partnerships

Establishing and fostering partnerships is a vital component of effective school leadership. Throughout the internship, you are expected to develop a variety of projects that contribute to the overall functioning of the school that promotes student success. Often, these projects require partnering with various organizations, both internal to your district as well as external agencies. These projects can serve as the foundation for future administrative positions and provide a wealth of positive networking opportunities for you with community partners. Within this section, we will review some of the central tenets to effective partnerships with external agencies that include understanding communication and interaction with partners, the benefits of partnerships, and considerations for planning out the partnerships.

Effective Partnerships

Schools and districts are open systems that regularly interact with the external community. We know that schools, communities, and families connect together in a variety of ways to maximize learning and social opportunities for students. Good leaders recognize the value external partners bring to schools. We rely on strong partnerships to provide a variety of resources and opportunities for students that are not generally available through regular district means. These may include activities such as tutoring, civic engagement for students, parent involvement opportunities, donations of school supplies, and service learning projects for students.

Partnerships are beneficial for students, the school, the district, and the partners themselves. When you begin exploring a partnership with an agency, you should be aware that there are many ways the school itself can support the partner, rather than merely the partner aiding the school. This should be taken into consideration when you speak with potential partners.

Recognizing the various types of partners we can connect with as leaders enables us to open up a door of possibilities that would not generally be an option for our schools. The types of partners available to you and your school may vary depending on your school location. Urban school districts' partners may look vastly different from partners' districts in rural areas, and the same can be said of suburban partners. Part of your responsibility in your administrative internship is to identify the various partners that you can potentially connect with for your projects. This should be done early in your internship and before you begin planning out any projects. The best starting point is to generate a list based upon a conversation with the principal and other administrators at the building. Your principal may also refer you to others within your building, as well at your central office. As an aid, a list of potential partners is provided for your initial consideration:

- ◆ faith-based organizations
- ◆ civic organizations

- ◆ police department
- ◆ fire department
- ◆ social services
- ◆ the YMCA
- ◆ the city or county family engagement office
- ◆ military installations
- ◆ universities
- ◆ neighborhood organizations
- ◆ local businesses and not-for-profits

Once your list has been generated, it is good practice to learn about each of your potential partners. There may be materials available about the potential partners through your administrative liaisons. However, if there is not a resource that provides an overview of potential partners, you may consider undertaking a project that involves partner inventory as a part of your internship. More on the partner inventory is provided at the end.

Components of Effective Partnerships

There are many different considerations for crafting a partnership with an external organization. These include the aforementioned awareness of the organization itself, planning the partnership imitative, effective communication, and evaluating the partnership. The following section provides you considerations for each as you develop your internship activities with your external partners.

Planning

Effective internship activities are successful when they are well planned. Partners cannot be involved at the "last minute" in any initiative and therefore should be considered early on in the initiative planning process. A Collaborative Planning Framework (Mast, Scribner, & Sanzo, 2011) is a useful tool when considered the scope of your initiative in tandem with partners. The following Internship Partnership Planning Framework (adapted from Mast et al., 2011; Sanzo, 2016) may be used in this process.

Internship Partnership Planning Framework

Multiple viewpoints are involved in the planning.	Consider including multiple members of the partner organizations in the planning process, including members from your school in the planning initiative.
The process is values driven.	Take into account the values of both your own school as well as that of the partner when developing an initiative for your internship. These are critical when developing the partnership and for the sustainability of the initiative.

The planning process for the partnership discourages compartmentalization of efforts.	As an intern, you may be provided one or two substantive tasks to accomplish at your internship site. Keep in mind the various other initiatives that are already under way and look how you can "dovetail" activities to maximize capacity and resources. Compartmentalizing activities does not promote sustainability or effective implementation of an initiative.
There is a focus on consensus making.	The partnership initiative involves multiple stakeholders and as such there needs to be a consensus on the initiative, rather than one or two people driving the process forward without buy-in from all partners.
There is an acknowledgement of difference(s) in power.	Partnerships are inherently differential in the intensity of effort by various stakeholders. This does not mean one partner is valued more or less than others, rather an acknowledgement of the differences in time, energy, and effort by different partners.

Effective Communication

The best collaborations are ones where there is an established line of communication. When you are working on your internship initiative with partners, ensure that you know who the contact is for the organization. Even if you are working with other people within the organization, that "lead communicator" should be included in everything to promote clear lines of communication and avoid either duplicitous or conflicting messages. It is also good practice early in the partnership to articulate the specific roles and responsibilities of each partner.

Evaluating the Partnership Effort

In your internship, you will be a part of many different opportunities and initiatives. Any effort that you have designed or co-designed should include an evaluative component. This not only provides ongoing feedback for you as your program evolves, but also demonstrates to a potential employer your ability to develop and implement an effective program evaluation. An evaluation report detailing the program itself and outcomes for your partners are also very helpful in continuing to support effectives long-term partnerships for your school.

School Partnership Activities

Place an "X" by the activity or activities below that are approved or required by your school and university supervisor as part of your intern plan. You must choose at least ONE activity in this area but a majority to all of the activities are recommended for maximum learning and experience.

   a) After-School Mentoring: Partner with a local community center to lead an after-school mentoring program.
   b) After-School Enrichment Program: Develop an after-school enrichment program with community partners to focus on

engaging activities for students, such as a chess club, art club, or other creative experiences for students, capitalizing on the backgrounds of your stakeholder partners.

c) Business Shadowing: Develop a program where middle and high school students can shadow business partners for a day to learn in-depth about their careers.

d) Career Fair: Bring in community partners for a career fair to expose students to a variety of potential career opportunities.

e) Dual College Credit: Partner with a local university or community college to design and oversee programs for high school students to acquire college credits.

f) Community Reads: Connect with community members to come into elementary classrooms and volunteer to read to classes and/or in small groups with students.

g) Educational Camps: Partner with a local Big Brothers/Big Sisters organization to run educational camps during school breaks for students.

h) General Educational Development (GED) Test Coordination: Partner with local churches or civic organizations to coordinate the GED program.

i) Partner Inventory: It is extremely helpful to have an inventory of potential external partners. This inventory can provide you and other leaders an overview of the partner, the organization leaders/contacts, and a general understanding of the collaborative potential. Items to consider in the inventory include:

- general description of the organization
- organization contact information (person, email, phone)
- past and current collaborations with the school
- resources of the organization
- possible collaborative initiatives

j) Technical Assistance Coordination: Partner with your state department of education to design and lead technical assistance trainings for schools. Specific schools for this can include those who are in or near school improvement.

k) Testing Coordinator: Collaborate with the state test developer (e.g., Pearson, ETS, etc.) to assist in overseeing testing administration. This can be administration in general or administration related to special considerations for testing.

- Other related activities approved by your supervisor, and/or service activities to district/school assigned by the supervisor, and/or activities that are part of a larger project.

51. Reflection in Action

In writing this section on reflection, we tried to respond to the notion that reflection is built into all of the assignments in the internship text, as well as into the coursework that readers will be experiencing throughout their graduate programs. We believe it will be helpful to define reflection and reflective practices in order to understand how reflection is part of administrative learning.

Defining Reflection and Reflective Practice

Reflection means looking at practice systematically. Principal interns and novice administrators need to understand how reflection is different from other types of thought. What is it that we are looking for when we look at evidence of reflection and reflective skills? How does reflection compare with other terms such as inquiry, critical thinking, and metacognition, which are often associated with reflective practice? One problem is that reflection has come to mean everything to everybody and as a result has lost some of its ability to mean anything. Rodgers (2002) argues that without some greater precision for the term, reflection will be dismissed because no one will know what to look for, what to observe in practice, or ultimately what to assess.

To gain a deeper understanding of the meaning of reflection, Rogers cites Dewey (1933) and provides readers with four definitions for reflection:

- ♦ Reflection is meaning-making; it moves the learner to a deeper understanding of experience and its relationship with and connections to other experiences and ideas;
- ♦ Reflection is systemic, rigorous, and disciplined ways of thinking with roots in scientific inquiry;
- ♦ Reflection is part of a community of learners, understood in interaction with others; and
- ♦ Reflection is an attitude that values the personal and intellectual growth of oneself and others.

(Rodgers, 2002, p. 245)

Reflection as Meaning Making. School administrators and practitioners are sometimes accused of having an experience but missing its meaning. Administrators, by definition, engage with others in the world. They need to make sense of new events, based on a repertoire of previous experiences. Researchers indicate they "stand on the shoulders of giants" to imply that understanding is built around consensus and that learning from one source is applied in subsequent situations. Chess players gain expertise from the experiences of studying thousands of unique situations, which are then recalled and applied in new circumstances. Administrative practice is context bound and every situation has unique qualities, which must be considered in order to take action.

Experience, by itself, is not enough; actions can become routinized or one can become cynical. The goal of reflection is to learn what to take away from one's experiences. Reflective practitioners learn from experience by connecting their individual and personal experiences with deeper and more extended considerations that are raised by knowledgeable others. "The creation of meaning out of experience is at the very heart of what it means to be human. It enables us to make sense of and attribute values to the events of our lives" (Rodgers, 2002, p. 848).

Reflection as Rigorous Way of Thinking. Reflection is more than stream of consciousness or simply believing that something is the case; it is systematic and disciplined (Rodgers, 2002). Reflection bridges one experience to the next by moving a practitioner from a state of questioning (perplexity) to a more settled state, when the implications of experiences are not yet fully established. This process involves a certain amount of curiosity, which opens up the possibility of new learning.

Reflection as Part of a Community of Learners. Reflection is not something that is done in isolation, but occurs in a community of learners. Reflecting on experience, on what happened, requires that other people are involved in the learning. There is need to verbalize and unpack the given circumstances of an event, what happened, and what may need to be done differently in the future. Otherwise, one risks repeating the same mistakes over and over and missing the meaning of one's experiences, instead of learning from experience.

Reflection as a Set of Attitudes. Learning is more than a cognitive process and also involves attitudes, feelings, and emotions. Reflection encompasses attitudes about how to embrace one's experiences: 1) wholeheartedness in embracing one's experiences, 2) directness in scrutinizing one's own performance, 3) open-mindedness for new ways of seeing and understanding events, and 4) readiness to be curious and grow through reflection.

Ultimately, reflection is not an end to itself, but a tool to connect everyday experiences into meaning-filled theory, which serves larger purposes of individual moral growth and societal change. Reflection is disciplined thinking and can be practiced, assessed, and perfected if learners are expected to grow from their experiences on the job and in life (Rodgers, 2002, p. 864).

Reflection In-Action and On-Action

How does one use the activities and assignments experienced during the internship to become a more effective principal? The simple answer is that one learns by reflecting on their experiences. So far, however, we have considered the process of reflection as an after-the-fact reconstruction of experience, *reflection-on-action*. Reflection-on-action is "the ordered, deliberate, and systematic application of logic to a problem in order to resolve it" (Russell & Munby, 1991, p. 165).

There is also a second and distinct process that Russell and Munby point to, in which practitioners adjust the ways they hear and see events, in the moment, and make adjustments accordingly. These moments are described as *reflections-in-action* and are more akin to the gestalt shifts that people experience when looking at the reversible pictures of the "old woman or young lady" or "duck or rabbit" (Gestalt Shift, 1998). The essence of reflection-in-action is in "hearing" or "seeing" things differently. For Schön (1991), this process is also called *reframing*, the application of learning to what is taught by experience. New actions and new frames go hand in hand; when administrators try new things, they reframe their prior experiences. Their professional knowledge draws from experience *and* the application of theory, from rethinking and talking through one's experiences. Effective administrators move back and forth between the "know-how" that is found in their actions, and the formal, symbolic explanations or representations of those actions. It is not one or the other, but the goal is for you to move back and forth between the two, between action and reflection, in order to gain a deeper understanding of your administrative practices.

Learning Reflective Practice

Learning reflective practice is one of the goals of your internship experience. Taylor, Rudolf, and Goldy (2008) define three core stages for learning reflective practice: 1) understanding the social construction of reality, 2) recognizing one's own contribution to that construction, and 3) taking action to reshape that construction (p. 659). Understanding the social construction of reality suggests that our internal perceptions shape how we view external reality. In other words, your own inner thoughts and prior experiences shape how define situations and make inferences. Recognizing your own contribution to that construction moves away from making premature inferences and begins the more detailed and labor-intensive work of describing what is going on in a given situation. Taking action requires a reframing of an event in ways that alter your previous construction, in words and actions that move away from focusing on why things happen and instead provide richer and more detailed explanations for how things work in the world. It should also be clear that the three concepts are not separate from one another, and there is constant intermingling of them. You may find it useful, however, to identify them separately, in order to break established patterns of seeing and acting.

Logs and Other Tools for Reflection Activities in the Internship

As mentioned earlier, reflection is critical in leadership preparation, both as a means of learning about practice and developing a leadership perspective and as a leadership skill for problem solving, innovation, and continuous learning. Reflective practice enables candidates to learn from their field experience through examining what they did or what happened and surfacing and examining the related values and assumptions. By stepping back and reflecting upon what was learned through hands-on experience, what worked or did not work, and how course readings, experiences, and other theory and research might inform the work, candidates gain insight into understanding the nature of school and district leadership and their own leadership skill development and proficiency.

The internship provides many opportunities for reflection, about the experiences interns have and with others who support their leadership development. This includes a university advisor, internship supervisor, and peers, all of whom can participate in reflection on practice for and with the intern.

Reflection on experience must be structured to facilitate learning (Schön, 1987, 1991). The key elements to the reflection-in-action cycle are to identify key experiences; analyze and reflect on the actions, values, and assumptions; formulate concepts and draw generalizations about leadership practices; and test these out in new situations for further reflection on action (Kolb, 1984). To support this process, interns need to document their internship experiences systemically, as these occur through logs or other means of recording. Structured questions can facilitate interns' analysis on the actions and help to surface their assumptions. Further self-analysis or discussions with supervisors and peers can help interns draw out lessons and meanings, consider alternative perspectives, and develop new ideas about leadership practice to try out in the future. This reflection on experience should occur concurrently with the internship as a formative process and can also occur at the end of an internship as a summative learning opportunity. Below are descriptions of commonly used tools and resources to facilitate reflection about the internship experience.

Log. The internship log is a record of the intern's experiences and should be used to summarize each primary activity performed; it details the hours and dates, intern's role, and products or artifacts. As an initial step in analyzing their experiences, interns can identify the leadership standards and indicators that correspond to their internship activities. Completed logs should be shared with the university advisor on a regular basis (such as weekly or monthly). An analysis of the logs can identify support oversight of the interns' experience by helping to track internship breadth, depth, alignment to leadership standards, and leadership development progress. Interns then may select specific activities or experiences for reflection-on-action or be encouraged by their university advisor to do so.

Reflection Journal. Interns should keep a reflective journal of their building-level internship experiences. Through these, interns can observe and evaluate the significance of their internship activities for personal growth, leadership skill development, and achievement of school and district goals. The reflective journal can also be a means for recording and examining practical and ethical dilemmas and considering alternatives. Interns' reflections should relate their experiences to the program's leadership standards (such as state or national standards) and course readings as appropriate. The reflections should raise ideas about how an intern might alter or improve their skills or a leadership dilemma in the future. Taken together, a good reflection shows evidence of reflective skills in application, analysis, synthesis, and evaluation.

The following questions can be useful guides for reflective journal entries:

1) What are you learning about your leadership style, strengths, and/ or development areas?
2) What are you learning about diversity (for example, but not limited to, race, culture, and language diversity, diversity of thought, diversity of educational approach) and your own work related to diversity? What were your opportunities to address issues of equity or reduce disparities that may exist? What do you observe others doing?
3) What is instructional leadership? What are you learning about the connection between leadership and improving student learning and achievement? What do you observe others doing and what have you been able to do?
4) How does a school leader develop and support a unifying vision for student achievement and school improvement? What are the challenges and limitations?
5) What challenging leadership situations or leadership opportunities have you experienced and how have you addressed them? What did you learn and how might you address the situation or opportunity differently as a leader?
6) What examples of best practice have you observed and how might you build upon those practices in your own leadership work?

It is recommended that interns complete at least two journal entries per week. Reflective journals should be submitted to the university-based internship supervisor regularly to foster the cycle of reflective inquiry about practice.

Conference Groups or Internship Seminars. Reflection is enhanced as a conversation or discussion with others who can help raise questions, challenge assumptions, and promote alternative explanations or directions. Thus, interns' learning and development through their internship is enhanced through reflection with others – supervisors, advisors, or peers – in small group forums, such as conference groups of six to eight interns meeting with an advisor, or an internship seminar, with an instructor and a cohort of peers (often 15–25 interns). These can be structured, using protocols and other discussion tools (McDonald, Mohr, & Dichter, 2007) to promote critical inquiry about internship experiences, challenges, and assumptions.

Summative Reflection. At the end of the internship experience, interns should be encouraged to reflect about their leadership development as it progressed from the beginning to the end. This reflection should enable them to identify how and in what ways their leadership skills developed and what experiences were most influential and how. They should also reflect on how their ideas and assumptions of leadership and school improvement has shifted and in what ways. Finally, they should be able to identify their challenges and areas for improvement and how they propose to continue their leadership development, particularly through reflective practice about their work.

52. Ethical and Critical Reasoning

In the following section, you will be given scenarios and activities to assist you in applying and reflecting on your own learning. After reading each case scenario, follow the steps outlined in the situation or setting. The goal is to continue developing your own capacity for reflective practice by following the questions and steps outlined in each scenario or situation.

The Power of Vision

Effective principals set high learning standards for all children to achieve. They have a clear vision of what they want to accomplish, possess high ethical standards and strong values, and have a sound set of beliefs on which to base all education policies, decisions, and actions. Effective principals know how to enlist the support of all school stakeholders to collaborate in the development of a rich, productive environment for teaching and learning in the school. This is a critical goal to achieve, because the most important factor in providing successful education programs and practices is faithful adherence to a strong set of values and beliefs together with a shared vision. There is no question that the basic philosophy, spirit, and drive of a unified administration, faculty, staff, and community have far more to do with successfully educating all children than do technology or economic resources, organizational structure, or innovation. All of these factors weigh heavily on success; however, they are transcended by how strongly the principal, faculty, and staff believe in basic precepts and how faithfully they carry them out.

Critical Reasoning and Ethics: Points to Ponder

1. Is there evidence to indicate that the leadership in my school adheres to a clear set of high ethical values and beliefs?
2. Does the leadership in my school understand and use research to facilitate a positive climate for continuous ongoing professional development for faculty and staff?
3. Do the education leaders in my school demonstrate a commitment to a premise that all students must be educated to achieve success in adult life?
4. How effective is the leadership in my school at articulating a clear vision for successful schooling and in setting high standards for learning?

5. To what extent are the faculty and staff in my school committed to supporting high learning standards for all children and abiding a shared vision?
6. Do community stakeholders support high learning standards and the school vision?

Summative Task

1. Write a vision statement for a school; discuss it with your site mentor and the university supervisor – or with a school leadership team for evaluation and feedback.
2. Show how community and school stakeholders participated in the development of the vision.
3. Collect, interpret, and analyze school data and draft a set of recommendations to serve as a guide for school improvement.
4. Convene a group of your peers to discuss your work and ask for critical feedback.
5. Meet with a few community stakeholders to get their perspectives and gain additional feedback.
6. Write a reflective paper summarizing what you learned.
7. File your responses in your notebook or e-portfolio for future reflection and reference.

Successful Leaders Focus on Vision, Quality, Equity, and Caring

A learning-centered leader knows that successfully educating children requires a sustained collaborative effort on the part of the board of education, community, faculty, staff, and administration. Assuring that all children reach a high level of academic achievement is made possible when the leadership possesses the ability to articulate, support, and sustain a vision clearly focused on quality education, equity, and caring. Successful educational leaders are able to lead the school/community stakeholders in the development of a clear vision, mission, and goals to serve as a guide for the education of children. They lead in the development of a positive environment for teaching and learning. They create a safe harbor for the free exchange of ideas regarding what is required to successfully educate all children to live a lifetime of success as adults. Learning-centered leaders know that faculty, staff, administration, and students will stay clearly focused on accomplishing the vision – as well as important education goals and high student achievement for all – only to the degree that the leadership is firmly committed to the premise that success for all is an absolute must. Learning-centered learners produce the best results by practicing the following principles: (a) The primary goal of successful educational leadership is high academic achievement for every student; (b) This lofty goal can be achieved when educators take genuine pride in the academic growth of all children; and (c) Leaders, educators, and children must be able to experience feelings of accomplishment and joy in their work. Note: Fear of failure must be expunged from the school environment. The mistaken beliefs that fear and sanctions represent effective motivation for either children or adults is wrong-headed thinking.

Critical Reasoning: Points to Ponder

1. To what extent is the leadership in your school focused on justice, fair play, ethics, equality, and academic achievement for all students? If it is not, why?
2. Is fear of failure and sanctions used to motivate students, faculty, staff, and administrators? If such behavior exists in the school, what would you do to remedy the problem?
3. Does my school use high-stakes testing to measure academic achievement?
4. What plan is in place to accommodate the wide variety of special needs, cultural considerations, ethnicities, and socioeconomic needs that predominate in my school?
5. To what extent is the leadership of my school concerned with issues of social competency and high achievement for all concerned?
6. What insights, concerns, or questions do you have regarding this statement?

Summative Task

1. How would you go about articulating a clear vision for the school that promotes high learning standards and academic achievement for all children?
2. Meet with a school administrator to discuss the kinds of skills and attributes necessary to implement, support, and sustain a clear vision of teaching and learning in the school.
3. Assess the degree to which both quantitative and qualitative data-based research and strategic planning are focused on addressing the educational needs of children in the school.
4. Develop a school improvement plan that communicates a clear vision of academic success for all children to school staff, students, parents, and community.
5. Discuss the plan with your mentor to gain additional insight.
6. Meet with a group of peers, parents, and the public to discuss what they think needs to be done to provide better learning opportunities for children. Take care to listen critically to all input and consider how you would go about infusing their input into school improvement plans.
7. Write a reflective paper on what you learned and how you can use the learning to complement your leadership.
8. File responses in your notebook for future reflection and reference.

The Principal and Teacher Evaluation

The primary purpose of teacher evaluation is to improve performance, as well as to measure teacher effectiveness. Most school districts have well-developed policies, procedures, and teacher evaluation instruments for principals to employ in the process of evaluating teachers. The successful principal takes care to publish the school district's established teaching standards to inform all concerned about the criteria by which teachers will be evaluated. He/she notifies the teachers prior to conducting performance evaluations in order for them to be fully prepared to demonstrate the level of their teaching competency. During the course of the evaluation, the principal documents the teacher's instructional performance, taking care to identify both strong points and any limitations that may be observed. He/she conferences with the teacher after each evaluation session to determine what the teacher thought about his/her performance, as well as what might have been done differently to help ensure that all of the students in the class achieve the learning objective/s set forth in the lesson. Once the teacher and the principal share their individual perspectives regarding the teacher's performance, they must collaborate to craft a teacher improvement plan. The plan may include mentoring, coaching, and employing best practice relevant to the specific improvements noted.

A typical teacher improvement plan includes the following components:

- Fairness and ethical considerations, which dominate teacher improvement plans.
- Areas identified as needing improvement are based on evaluation results.
- Teachers are provided with an opportunity to rebut negative evaluations or request that an additional evaluation be conducted by another qualified evaluator in the school or district.
- Teachers are provided with an adequate period of time to bring their performance up to the district's established teaching standards.
- Teachers are provided with the administrative support, resources, and mentoring required to make the required improvements.
- The principal and teacher schedule a subsequent teacher evaluation session to measure progress made toward meeting the district's established teaching standards.

Note: Exemplary teaching performance must be recognized and rewarded. Subpar teaching performance must be documented and appropriate corrective action taken to remediate inadequate performance. The successful principal knows that doing anything less is simply not acceptable.

Critical Reasoning: Points to Ponder
1. How strongly does the leadership in your school support the use of proven teaching methods, theories, and relevant curricula to promote academic success for all students?

2. Does your school employ a well-organized plan for teacher evaluation and ongoing professional growth and development?
3. Is teacher evaluation in your school based on established teaching standards?
4. Is teacher evaluation in your school used to improve teaching and learning?
5. Is the evaluation of teachers in your school fair, based on established teaching standards, and in compliance with ethical considerations, law, and district policy and procedures?
6. What questions, concerns, or ideas do you have about the effectiveness of teaching and learning in your school?
7. What changes would you make to enhance student achievement for all students?

Summative Task

1. Discuss the teacher evaluation with a respected school administrator; inquire about current research and best practice relevant to teaching, learning, and assessment to gain additional insight.
2. Discuss the importance of new teacher induction, mentoring, and the appropriate use of best practice to facilitate professional development.
3. Look for evidence that good behavior, respect for all, and ethical considerations help inform the evaluation of teachers in your school.
4. Develop a written response; describe what you learned and how you can use the learning as a school leader.
5. File your response in your portfolio for future reflection and reference.

Making Ethical Decisions

There are several critical components a leader must consider during the decision-making process if he/she expects the school/community stake-holders to support whatever he/she decides is the best course of action to take. Some leadership decisions are fairly easy to make, because certain legal aspects or board policy is the only alternative or the decision is clearly the best thing to do for students. However, there are times when deciding what to do is not so easy. There are instances when a leader has to choose a course of action from several alternative solutions, some of which may have only subtle differences. In addition, there are times when it may seem that a good solution does not exist. These kinds of troublesome situations put the leader in a very difficult position indeed! Arriving at a decision that others will support or at least accept can be made somewhat less contentious by understanding some of the factors that typically influence a leader's decision. If he/she doesn't know the personal factors that tend to drive his/her thoughts, decisions, and actions, he/she will more often than not see his/her decisions or actions come under serious fire from stakeholders. This is especially true whenever questions of ethics are involved. Fortunately, leaders who know their personal (perspectives) factors (perceptions) are in a better position to make the best possible decision, based on the best and most current information available during the deliberation process.

Here are some do's and don'ts that successful leaders use to guide their decisions and actions. First, work toward formulating a well-thought-out solution when faced with an unexpected or difficult problem. Never succumb to the temptation to make a hasty decision. A rush to judgment and/or deciding an issue based on one's initial reaction is a sure pathway to failure. Obviously, a leader can't put off a decision indefinitely. However, all decisions must be carefully considered prior to implementation. Think about possible points of contention and prepare to address questions or concerns about the decision in an open, respectful way. This will go a long way toward having others accept a leader's course of action.

Second, provide appropriate transparency and prepare to address hard questions in a timely manner. They can't be permitted to sit and fester. Avoiding questions or inaction only serves to widen the scope of any conflict associated with deciding among competing solutions with no clear benefits.

Third, where two alternative solutions are present, there is a good chance that one of them will be selected for implementation because of the need for closure. This can cause serious trouble for a leader, especially when neither solution is very good. It is much better to take criticism for inaction than it is for choosing a poor solution.

Fourth, a good strategic approach to decision-making is to develop at least three alternative solutions for consideration, but be aware: Whenever a leader chooses one of the three alternatives under consideration, he/she may be tempted to select the simplest solution instead of one with more complexity. The fact that one solution is easier to comprehend than another does not mean that it is the best one. Selecting the simplest alternative solution, especially when it doesn't address the root cause of a problem, can make a leader look weak, ineffective, or, worse, incompetent. A leader needs to carefully examine each alternative solution closely – through an ethical lens – to determine which one is the best fit to help resolve a problem. One way to accomplish this outcome is to render each alternative solution to its simplest form before deciding what to do. A decision grounded on ethical considerations makes the solution easier for all concerned to understand and support.

Fifth, a leader faced with too many alternative solutions may find it very difficult to make a decision. In these situations, a leader should work to reduce the number of alternatives. An effective way to reduce the number of alternatives is to search the literature on the matter, invite stakeholder input, and use the information to help limit the number of alternatives to a more workable number. This process provides the leader with additional information, enhances transparency, and typically generates broader stakeholder support for the final decision.

The most successful leader knows that stakeholders may have a vested interest in the decisions and actions he/she makes. How he/she decides is as important to stakeholders as what he/she decides.

Critical Reasoning: Points to Ponder
- An effective leader is fair and just. Everyone is treated equally.
- An effective leader develops listening skills. There is value in the input of others.
- An effective leader is honest and transparent, no matter how popular or unpopular.
- An effective leader makes sure all decisions are in accordance with policy, the law, and high ethical standards.
- An effective leader always leads by example.
- What can you do to make sure your leadership reflects these characteristics and attributes?

Summative Task
Meet with a trusted school leader to discuss ethics and leadership. Ask how he/she copes with ethical issues during the process of making difficult decisions under the watchful eye of the public.

1. Convene a group of your peers to discuss their perceptions of ethics and leadership. Ask how they think a leader can enhance his/her reputation for honesty, integrity, and credibility when dealing with ethical issues.
2. Make a point to closely observe leadership behaviors during meetings. Identify areas where leadership behaviors might generate trust, confidence, and stakeholder support. Also, make note of how leadership behaviors might be improved.
3. Set aside time to reflect on what you learned by observing and discussing ethical considerations with others. Ask yourself what you learned and how you might be able to use what you learned to assure that your leadership meets high ethical standards.
4. Write a reflective piece and file it in your portfolio for future reference.

Preserving Ethics: An Essential Component in Leadership
School leaders today face close scrutiny from a wider range of stakeholders than ever before. The reality is that school administrators today have more people closely monitoring their decisions and actions to make sure what the leadership does is legal, moral, and ethical. Deciding the legality of a school issue is fairly straightforward and in the main a perfunctory task. There are

education laws, statutes, policies, rules, and regulations promulgated by the state and other relevant governing bodies upon which school leaders can rely to help inform administrative decisions or actions. In situations where the law may seem fuzzy or uncertain to the leadership, school attorneys are typically available to provide clarity or aid the administrator in making decisions that are compliant with the law.

Most school leaders don't have much difficulty making decisions or taking action in matters involving morality. Community values, mores, culture, and peer pressures are ever present in schools. These components help serve as an effective guide to school leaders wrestling to resolve important issues in ways that the public will deem just, equitable, and morally acceptable. Making sound ethical decisions is a bit more complicated. Some of the most troublesome issues school leaders face will fall into gray areas, which are not easily defined as right or wrong, legal or illegal, moral or immoral. Nevertheless, an ethical issue is sure to capture the attention of the public to the point where it may seem as if the whole community is watching every step the leader takes. The truth is that blinding rays of light are sharply trained on school leadership, with the public standing by to make sure the leadership decisions or actions taken will meet the public's ethical standards.

The successful school leader knows ethics will hold sway whenever the law and morality move off center stage, where questions may not be governed by the clear, bright lines provided by law or doctrines of right or wrong, fair, or just. Ethics can create an uncertain, even a volatile, environment for school leaders. While they may not face incarceration or pay fines for violating professional ethics, as is the case with breaking the law or committing a moral transgression, leaders who act in unethical ways will pay a heavy cost in terms of losing the respect, trust, and confidence of all concerned. This can render their ability to lead extremely difficult, if not impossible. Indeed, one unethical act can derail the career of even the most effective school leader.

The most successful school leaders know that avoiding ethical missteps begins with understanding that the leader's relationship with one affects his/her relationships with everyone. If people perceive that the leader plays favorites or caters to certain persons deemed to have influence or power, they are sure to lose confidence in his/her ability to lead. On the other hand, when a leader is viewed as honest, transparent in his/her dealings with others, and demonstrating a genuine commitment to decide matters with respect, fairness, equity, and acceptability, he/she is perceived to be trustworthy. Fortunately, successfully navigating through issues involving ethics can be enhanced by understanding the troubled waters associated with leadership and ethical considerations.

1. Schools are public agencies and as such derive power from the state, creating a local political system wherein politics are ever-present and driven by power and influence.

2. People are keenly aware that power and influence are subject to abuse by those in power, which therefore justifies public scrutiny.
3. Left unchecked, abuse of power and influence by leaders will result in an environment where favoritism, nepotism, conflict of interest, misuse of scarce resources, and/or marginalizing certain groups or individuals predominate the organization. Consequently, the abuse generates suspicion, distrust, and, finally, a loss of public confidence and support.

Critical Reasoning: Points to Ponder
1. Have I considered the consequences of my decisions?
2. Am I aware of people's perception of me? If necessary, do I need to adjust my behavior?
3. Do I put my ego and my own interests behind the interest of the community I serve?
4. What can I do to assure that my actions, behaviors, and decisions meet high ethical standards?

Summative Task
1. Meet with a trusted school leader to discuss ethics and leadership. Ask how he/she copes with ethical issues during the process of making difficult decisions under the watchful eye of the public.
2. Convene a group of your peers to discuss their perceptions of ethics and leadership. Ask how they think a leader can enhance his/her reputation for honesty, integrity, and credibility when dealing with ethical issues.
3. Make a point to closely observe leadership behaviors during meetings. Identify areas where leadership behaviors might generate trust, confidence, and stakeholder support. Also, make note of how leadership behaviors might be improved.
4. Set aside time to reflect on what you learned by observing and discussing ethical considerations with others. Ask yourself what you learned and how you might be able to use what you learned to assure that your leadership meets high ethical standards.
5. Write a reflective piece and file it in your portfolio for future reference.

How to Avoid Ethical Traps
An ethical act may be viewed as unethical because of the way it's handled or because detractors put a negative spin on the outcome. An honest, well-intended act can be characterized as inappropriate, self-serving, or unethical if it lacks transparency or if the leadership assumes a stance of superiority. This situation becomes very serious during times of unrest, which typically occur when the leadership must consider critical issues, such as a promotion, reduction in force, and the reassignment or termination of personnel. There

may be legitimate reasons why quick action is necessary or only a limited number of people are permitted to participate in the decision, for example, certain legal issues, where confidential matters are at stake. However, the appearance of a lack of transparency can provide more than enough ammunition for school/community stakeholders to make life extremely problematic for the leadership.

Common Ethical Traps

1. Hiring decisions tend to be watched carefully by stakeholders. Most schools are the largest employer in the community, therefore, certain stakeholders tend to feel that they ought to have a say in employment decisions. The community may also believe local residents should be given first consideration to fill positions in the school. Having good, clear policies and procedures in place to govern employment decisions and insisting that all concerned abide those rules and guidelines – without exception – will go a long way toward assuring the public that the selection process was equitable and fair and that the most qualified person available was selected for the position.

2. Reassignment, promotion, and disciplinary or termination decisions also garner close stakeholder scrutiny. These issues can involve matters of confidence; therefore, much of what goes into making the final decision must by law and/or policy remain confidential. These kinds of issues are typically handled in executive sessions of the school board, which permits only selected parties to attend and participate in the deliberations. While deliberation and discussion of confidential issues may be conducted during an executive session of the school board, any final decision/action must be voted on at a board meeting open to the public. During such times, the question of trust, honesty, integrity, and ethics may be sorely tested.

3. Relationships or conflicts of interest can be of significant concern whenever employment contracts, promotions, or major procurement decisions are made. Thinking about the types of questions the public may have regarding these decisions can help a leader avoid having his/her decision characterized as unethical. Examples of common questions stakeholders may have include, but are not limited, to the following:

   ♦ Did family connections or political influence drive the decision to hire or promote an individual?
   ♦ Did power, influence, or special interest pressure result in the awarding a major contract to provide goods and services to the school?

- Did some agency or vendor lose out on a contract because of political influence or favoritism?
- Was the decision-making process guided by applicable law and policy?
- Was the process as transparent as may be permitted by the applicable legal aspects of school governance and administration?

These are important questions for the leadership to address and prepare to answer before a decision is made, because public perceptions of bias can make even the fairest of decisions appear to be self-serving or unjust. Sadly, some leaders ignore unethical behaviors. They fail to speak up, mistakenly thinking it's not worth it to question the motivation behind inappropriate acts, it's not going to make a difference, or, worse, objecting to unethical behavior might have a negative impact on their career. Trustworthy leaders find public support for their decisions and actions, while leaders viewed as secretive, arrogant, or self-serving do not.

Critical Reasoning: Points to Ponder
Take a close look at the ways in which meetings are conducted and high-stake decisions are made in your school. Ask yourself:

1. Did the leadership provide adequate notice prior to the meeting so interested stakeholders could attend?
2. Did the leadership limit their comments to the items listed on the meeting agenda?
3. During meetings, do the leaders speak clearly and distinctly in order for the audience to easily follow discussions?
4. If questions of conflict of interest or special interest (real or imagined) were present, were they addressed or ignored?
5. Were communications between the leaders presented in a logical, well-organized manner?
6. Is the decision-making process responsibly transparent?
7. Does bias or favoritism seem to drive important decisions in the school?
8. Does the leadership demonstrate that he/she respects others and their ideas, especially whenever they may disagree with him/her?
9. Is stakeholder input given serious consideration during the decision-making process?
10. Are confidential issues protected as may be required, or do certain individuals seem to have inappropriate access to inside information?
11. Does the leadership appear to be a "know it all," arrogant, or dictatorial when making controversial decisions?
12. What is the level of trust between the faculty, staff, and school leadership?

13. What is the level of trust between the school leadership and the community?

14. What improvements, if any, do you think need to be made in these areas?

Summative Task

1. Meet with a couple of trusted leaders in the school and community to get their perspective on these questions. Listen for evidence that their response is centered on clear, rational thinking and relevant data. Make note of any difference between their observations and yours.

2. Convene a meeting of your peers to discuss the decision-making process in the school. Look carefully at the questions or concerns expressed. If perceptions of unethical behavior, favoritism, lack of trust, superiority, or fear are voiced, ask the attendees what might be done to rectify the situation.

3. Take time to think deeply on what you learned by completing this exercise. Critique your decision-making skills to ascertain areas of strength and limitations and identify areas needing improvement. Develop a written plan listing core leadership principles you can use to help improve the levels of trust and confidence in the school and community.

4. Write a reflective piece and file it in your portfolio for future reference.

The Principal and Ethical Behavior

As we think about the importance of a person, such as a principal, teacher, doctor, accountant, police officer, etc., being set apart to accomplish a public purpose, we would do well to keep in mind that good ethical behavior is a leadership must. In fact, we don't look kindly on the exceptions. Perhaps this is because we depend on others to abide by rules of good ethical behavior, just as they depend on us. Most of us do not violate rules of good behavior or ignore the laws or public policy set forth so that we may enjoy a safe, orderly society. While we may reserve the right to complain about rules, policy, or the law, few of us knowingly seek to evade our responsibilities. We trust. We trust our neighbor, accountant, banker, attorney, and the pilot of our plane. Experience may make us cautious concerning human failure and those exceptions when our trust might have been shaken. But that is the point: these are exceptions.

When taking on the role of school leadership, we become something more than ourselves. We carry the dreams and the hopes people have for their children. This is worth keeping in mind as we prepare and work toward providing effective leadership in our school, community, and nation. The bottom line is that as a principal, we must be fully committed to setting and demonstrating high standards of ethical behavior in our school and community.

Critical Reasoning: Points to Ponder

1. How effective is the leadership in your school with regard to setting and abiding by high standards of ethical behavior for all concerned?
2. What role does ethical behavior play in garnering public trust and support for the school?
3. What could you do to help assure that others view you as a model for good ethical behavior?
4. What questions, concerns, or ideas do you have regarding leadership and ethics?

Summative Task

1. Reflect on the relationship among communications, ethics, and effective leadership.
2. Discuss the topic with a respected school leader to gain additional insight.
3. Attend a community meeting, a faculty meeting, and at least one meeting of the governing board.
4. During meetings, did the leaders speak clearly and distinctly in order for the audience to easily follow discussions?
5. Did the leadership demonstrate respect for all concerned?
6. Did the leadership limit their comments to the items listed on the meeting agenda?
7. Did the leadership use data rather than personal beliefs or opinions to help formulate decisions and actions?
8. Did the leadership take care to decide matters according to established policy, rules, and regulations?
9. Were communications between the leaders presented in a logical, well-organized manner?
10. Did the leaders model ethics, enhance trust, and show respect for the organization?
11. Develop a written response, describe what you learned and how you can use the learning, and file a copy in your portfolio.

2.3 Service Activities

Education is a service profession. The intern should plan for appropriate modeling and accomplishments of service. The internship should balance the needs of the intern and the needs of the district/school. Care must be taken, however, that a realistic balance be maintained. The final plan should not be centered selfishly on your development, nor should you limit your experience by submitting totally to the specific needs or concerns of the district/school.

Service activities will come mainly from the site supervisor's recommendations. They can be written in the "Other" category listed under any of the 52 leadership areas. These may be assistance on current needs and projects, assistance with day-to-day administrative duties, or other needs that the site supervisor believes will benefit the district/school and the intern. The intern MAY NOT log more than four hours on any routine duty, e.g., bus, cafeteria, playground or hall duty, detention hall, etc.

2.4 Local Project Activity

The intern is required to conduct at least one local project. The project should be directly related to the district/school goals and related to the improvement of student performance. The project must:

- Include other faculty or staff in a group process
- Be led by the intern
- Have a plan that includes:
  1. Need for the project
  2. Goal of the project
  3. Resources available
  4. Timeline
  5. Method of evaluation
- Include skills used (e.g., decision-making, communication, etc.)
- Be approved by the supervisor

The intern may choose a large project or several smaller projects. It is strongly recommended that the size and number of projects be considered with respect to time needed to fulfill other activities and current job responsibilities. The action research project may be used to fulfill this requirement, but the intern is strongly advised to accept a leadership role in other projects.

2.5 Collaboration With the Site Supervisor

After completing Stage One and making preliminary choices of activities in the 52 skill and experience areas, meet with the site supervisor to reach consensus on a plan for the internship. The intern and site supervisor should discuss the intern's preferred activities and decide the nature of the service activities and the local project(s) described in sections 2.3 and 2.4 above. The plan should have adequate breadth and depth of activity in each of the ten professional standards to assess progress toward mastery.

2.6 Internship/Leadership Experience Overall Plan Report

In this activity, the intern will prepare and present an overall plan report. Typically, the intern will present to his/her supervisors, either as part of many reports by others or individually. The report must be a professional presentation, similar to reporting to the board. Documentation should include:

- Activities planned from the 52 leadership areas
- Service activities
- Action research and/or local project(s)
- List of resource persons to be used
- Estimated hours for the internship/leadership experience
- Estimated completion date

Implementation

Following final approval of the plan developed in Stage Two, the intern can begin implementing leadership activities. This stage describes further assistance and requirements during implementation.

3.1 Interviewing

It is highly recommended that the intern plan to schedule interviews with various school and community leaders. Interviews, however, should be only a small part of the overall experience. The vast majority of time should be spent working as opposed to observing or listening. Interviewing can affect several key outcomes that the intern should consider. These include:

- Meeting the right people and developing a network of experienced school leaders
- Knowing the various leadership positions and their responsibilities
- Providing the opportunity for current leaders to get to know you
- Forming new relationships – administrator to intern administrator, versus administrator to teacher/other
- Understanding different departments and perceptions from leaders and followers within each department
- Gaining insights into additional or more relevant internship activities
- Getting the "bigger picture" and having experienced mentors provide answers to questions/concerns from various areas and perspectives

Interview Questions

1) Tell me about your department/area.
2) Tell me about your job duties and responsibilities.
3) What are your strengths?
4) What are your goals?
5) What are your present major concerns?
6) What future concerns are anticipated?

7) What have you done to improve this school's capacity to better meet the needs of students?

8) What do you need, expect, or hope for from your principals?

9) From your experience of working with your district/school, what advice would you give a new principal?

10) What activities would you suggest I undertake during my internship to better understand and/or work with your department/area?

Add any additional questions appropriate to your knowledge/experience/ project need.

3.2 Networking

All leaders use networks to seek advice, discuss ideas, and improve their ability to fulfill the responsibilities of their positions. These networks often consist of mentors, coaches, peers, and experts in various fields. Contacts may also include community leaders, friends, and colleagues from professional and civic organizations.

The intern should keep a directory of key personnel used and any additional persons that he or she discovers during the internship. After choosing skill and experience activities, service activities, and local project(s), the intern should cite key persons that he or she plans to work with, interview, and/or use for help and assistance with his/her internship. Resource persons should give their permission and means of communication (phone, email, or times available). Some interns find it more efficient to collect and maintain a file of business cards. The documented resource network will be presented at the final internship summary report.

3.3 Essential Competencies of Leadership: Theory Into Practice

While Kurt Lewin was right to say, "there is nothing so practical as good theory," it is equally true that there is nothing so theoretical as good practice (Fullan, 2001a). Hoy and Miskel (2001) conclude that theory relates to practice in three ways: theory forms a frame of reference for the practitioner, theorizing provides for a general mode of analysis of practical events, and theory guides decision-making. Wise leaders realize the need to analyze the beliefs, dispositions, traditions, and experiences that form their theories of reality and guide their practice.

This section provides a brief overview of 12 essential competencies for leadership development. It is intended to provide a frame of reference for the intern to practice, reflect, and assess skill development. It is assumed that the intern has previous instruction and more in-depth study in each of these areas. Following each competency overview, a list of analysis questions is provided. Use these to analyze current performance and the development of future actions to address current problems encountered and assist in alleviating similar problems in the future. The 12 competencies are:

1. Developing trusting relationships
2. Leading in the realization of the vision
3. Making shared decisions
4. Communicating effectively
5. Resolving conflict and issues
6. Motivating and developing others
7. Managing group processes
8. Supporting others with appropriate leadership style
9. Using power ethically
10. Creating and managing a positive culture and climate
11. Initiating change
12. Evaluating student, personnel, and program performance

When problems occur or needs arise, people tend to focus on the immediate crisis. This focus may alleviate the current need, but does little to ensure that organizational learning has occurred or similar problems will occur less often. In these situations, leaders find themselves endlessly putting out the same types of fires. Consideration of each of the 12 competencies gives the leader the bigger picture and the necessary information to guide future actions for organizational improvement, heightened quality of life within the organization, increased learning, and the opportunity for developing self and others. In order to gather the necessary information, the leader has to ask the right questions to determine if competencies need development and improvement. The analysis questions provide for a more comprehensive definition of the problem and thus allow for more appropriate action.

Further analysis will assist in forming the proper mental framework for viewing real-life problems or needs. With enough practice, this framework of thinking becomes second nature to the leader. For optimal learning, it is advised that interns use real-life cases and cooperative learning groups. Greater learning occurs with the practice of analyzing and considering alternatives from a variety of perspectives. A sample case is provided in Appendix G to demonstrate how to analyze problems using reflective practice of leadership skill.

1. Developing Trusting Relationships

Covey (2009) believes there is one thing common to every individual and organization that, if removed, will destroy the best of organizations. He adds that if it is developed, it can bring unparalleled success. That one thing is trust. Green (2011) further noted that trust affects every relationship in your life and determines whether one realizes their dreams. He believes that without trust, true success is impossible. Trust is found in the vast majority of books on leadership to be crucial for success in leadership, if not the base of all leadership success.

Having confidence in the leader's honesty and ability has a great impact on the climate, culture, communications, and overall quality of life within the organization. Distrust breeds negativity, erases motivation, and is a major cause of turnover. Interns and new leaders must face the challenge of developing trusting relationships. Trust is not given with title or pay scale, but must be earned. This takes time and determined efforts to prove to others your reliability, honesty, and character. It can take years to earn trust, but it can be erased in a moment. The wise leader understands this and begins to take actions to build and sustain trust.

These actions include being honest in every dealing with others, following through with commitments, admitting mistakes, and knowing their strengths and limitations. They also initiate ways to truly know others and let others truly know them. They believe in individual worth and see individuals as teaching or directing the computer lab versus as faculty and staff. They view themselves as individuals leading versus a title or role. Being oneself does not require a role. Interns face broken relationships with other teachers as they move into administration. New relationships must be formed and new trust developed. Future school leaders must utilize research, practice, reflect, and form habits of developing and sustaining trusting relationships.

Analysis Questions for Trust

To what extent:

- ◆ Has trust through competence, honesty, and follow-through been established?
- ◆ Has the leader relied upon/trusted others?
- ◆ Is transparent leadership modeled in the school?

What actions need to be taken to address any concerns from above to solve the current problem and avoid similar problems in the future?

2. Leading in the Realization of the Vision

Of the popularly expressed requirements for leadership, one of the most common is that leaders have vision (Gardner, 1990). Vision is one aspect that the research has long held to separate leaders from administrators or managers. The administrative manager is one that "copes with complexity" or manages the current status quo, while the leader is "coping with" and initiating change (Kotter, 1998). Thus, mangers are concerned with the efficiency of the current system, while leaders look for greater effectiveness with new policies, procedures, and systems.

It is difficult to lead in schools today with many teachers and parents fearful of and resistant to change. It is equally difficult to lead the district or school when only those elected have the power to change. Additionally, beginning school administrators attempt to do things right and fulfill their job descriptions; they begin to behave like managers, not leaders. Realizing the vision involves risk, and few administrators are risk takers in their early years of administration.

Leaders strive to move the organization and all of its members to a new vision. Reducing risk and increasing the possibility of success for your vision requires all the other 11 competencies. The vision and the means to get there require understanding, effort, and support from the entire organization. They do not have to create the vision by themselves, but are responsible for providing the leadership for vision creation, articulation, and support. Future leaders must utilize research, practice, reflect, and form habits of developing and working toward the realization of the vision.

Analysis Questions for Vision
To what extent:

- Is there a clear vision of how the organization should be functioning now and in the future? Is it shared by all?
- Is the mission of the organization appropriate, understood, and supported?
- Has adequate planning and discussion occurred?
- Are the vision, mission, and plans aligned with the key principles and beliefs of those in the organization?
- Is the vision a broad-based, comprehensive picture of the processes, interactions, and accomplishments of all relevant stakeholders, i.e., students, teachers, parents, and administrators?

What actions need to be taken to address any concerns from above to solve the current problem and avoid similar problems in the future?

3. Making Shared Decisions
Decision-making is crucial to educational administration because the school, like all formal organizations, is basically a decision-making structure (Hoy & Miskel, 2001). Decision-making is a process that guides actions. Decisions are based on one's beliefs, values, and previous experiences. Leaders must know themselves, know why they choose particular paths, know whom to involve, and know which particular decision-making model to use.

It is assumed that the intern has deliberated on his/her key beliefs or principles and has some degree of understanding of the similarities and differences between themselves and others. He/she should continue to use reflection to make decisions: reflection will help the intern more fully understand the roots of his/her beliefs and the impact of those beliefs on decisions. This section will briefly review levels of involvement in shared decision-making.

Educational leadership has come a long way since the scientific management era in the early 20th century. Then, the ones at the top made the decisions and believed that a rational model would shape optimal decisions. They believed they could actually know all alternatives and predict the results of each alternative. Today, we know better. We know that those at the top cannot accurately gather or predict all alternatives. We know that followers deserve to be involved and better decisions are made with input and collaboration. The first decision is to decide what level of involvement is most effective.

Leaders have at least four options of involvement in decisions: *deciding alone, seeking participation and input, seeking collaboration,* and *letting others decide.* The wise leader uses participative and collaborative strategies for all-important decisions. However, this cannot always be done, nor should it always be done. The leader must assess five factors to decide on the level of involvement of others:

1. *Time.* Urgency may require the leader to decide for him/herself. Participative and collaborative decisions require more time. If important decisions are in need of more involvement, the leader must schedule additional time for greater involvement.
2. *Staff interest in the decision.* People differ in the things that interest them and the level of interest. For leaders desiring more participation or collaboration, interest in the decision must first be generated.
3. *Expertise of the staff.* At very low levels of expertise, followers typically accept the decisions of the leader and would have little to contribute. Leaders that desire greater collaboration, however, must raise levels of expertise in order to successfully involve subordinates.
4. *Importance or need for a high-quality decision.* Some decisions are much more important than others and carry significant consequences. This is almost always the case for instruction and learning, whether directly or indirectly. For important questions that demand a high-quality decision, greater participation or collaboration is needed.
5. *Degree of need for buy-in or support for the decision.* Many decisions in schools need the support of the staff for successful implementation and results. A collaborative model most often increases buy-in and support.

We live in a time of empowerment and involvement in decisions. The wise leader understands that better decisions are made with higher levels of involvement. This leader also understands that involvement does not simply happen or is always the best approach. Greater involvement and a collaborative (shared) decision model take time to plan, and it takes effort to educate and motivate staff to participate effectively. The resulting better decisions are worth the effort.

Analysis Questions for Decision-Making
To what extent:

  ♦ Was the appropriate decision-making model used?
  ♦ Were the major steps in decision-making followed?
  ♦ Was the appropriate level of involvement used?
  ♦ Were those affected by the decision included in the process?

What actions need to be taken to address any concerns from above to solve the current problem and avoid similar problems in the future?

4. Communicating Effectively
"Without exception, all major national school administration associations in this country stress the importance of effective communication skills" (Gorton & Snowden, 2002, p. 31). Despite these findings, schools are generally criticized for poor communication between leaders and faculty, teachers and other teachers, faculty and students, and school and community.

What do we know about communication? First, it is impossible for one person to imagine a concept or event, find the words or actions to describe (encode) it, relay these words or actions (transmit), and make another person understand (decode) the message exactly the way it was originally imagined. The difficulty of transmitting the feelings, impressions, and related experience unique to every individual only magnifies this dilemma. It is the leader's responsibility to continuously work toward more effective communication and better understanding among all individuals.

Second, we know that there are four major communication skill areas. The first is that leaders must be proficient in giving information. This includes oral, written, and technological information (email, web pages, Excel, PowerPoint, etc.). They must be highly proficient in the second area of communication: listening and receiving information. These two aspects of communication involve verbal and nonverbal strategies and cues. The successful leader develops both effective verbal and nonverbal behaviors.

In considering both giving and receiving information, a leader should emphasize receiving information. Covey (1989) found that successful leaders seek to understand before they seek to be understood. Listening and receiving information first allows the leader to have the whole picture, as opposed to giving information and allowing only others to know both sides and perspectives. Carnegie (1993) teaches that no one is more persuasive than a good listener. Listening results in many other positive outcomes. These include:

- Shows interest and respect for others
- Allows others to vent and models appropriate social skill
- Increases learning and understanding of other perspectives
- Critical for resolution of conflict
- Forms the habit and appearance of wisdom
- Allows time for observing others' information, e.g., body language, inflection, emotion, etc.
- Allows time for listening to what your mind, heart, emotion, and body are telling you
- Builds rapport and meaningful relationships
- Develops a culture of open communication

The third aspect of effective communication is the design and management of a communication system. Ultimately, the leader is responsible for communications within the organization and outside the organization. Without an effective system, the leader must depend on others for the accuracy and amount of information. This is often less than adequate because:

- Others often tell leaders only what they believe the leader wants to hear
- Others may tell the leader only the positive side
- Others may tell the leader only the negative side
- Others often omit vital information
- Many do not communicate with the leader

An effective communication system involves a variety of formats and avenues of communication. Successful leaders may regularly use meetings, surveys, interviews, group processes, suggestion boxes, needs assessments, open-door policies, the practice of walking the halls, eating in the cafeteria, and a host of others. The goal is to have enough means of communicating that allow different people to choose the format that they like and are willing to give and receive information. The breadth of avenues and formats also allow the leader to give and receive different types of communication.

The fourth and final aspect of communication is monitoring and evaluation of the first three, i.e., giving, receiving, and the system. Leaders must periodically evaluate the quantity and quality of the communication within the organization, as well as outside the organization. Future leaders must utilize research, practice, reflect, and form habits of effective communication.

Analysis Questions for Communication

To what extent:

- ◆ Did others infer my intended meaning?
- ◆ Have I fully understood what others are trying to say?
- ◆ Are people utilizing differing avenues of communication?
- ◆ Have I reached my entire intended audience?
- ◆ Is there a safe and open system for communication?

What actions need to be taken to address any concerns from above to solve the current problem and avoid similar problems in the future?

5. Resolving Conflict and Issues

Administrators are faced with classic disagreement between individual needs and organizational expectations; consequently, they spend a substantial amount of time attempting to mediate conflict (Hoy & Miskel, 2001). In self-assessments conducted in graduate leadership classes, the authors of this text found that most students initially avoided conflict. To the novice, this makes perfect sense – who wants to be in a conflict? The wise leader, however, views every conflict as an opportunity – an opportunity to improve the organizational effectiveness, improve the quality of life for some or all of its members, and better know and understand each other.

Conflict is inevitable and should warn the leader that a problem exists. Although unique situations may warrant different practices, the ideal approach is to problem-solve collaboratively. Kenneth Thomas (1976) identified five styles of managing conflict: *competing, collaborating, compromising, avoiding,* and *accommodating.* Competing is similar to a directive style, where a directive must be given, regardless of the competing belief. Compromising works well in the short-term, but it usually does not totally resolve the conflict. Accommodating is necessary when the leader is wrong or simply willing to give in to the other side. Avoiding is seldom recommended, except for buying time for things to "cool off" or gather additional information. The collaborating style uses problem-solving strategies and is the style most often recommended.

The two major areas of conflict facing leaders are conflict over differing expectations of roles and differing beliefs that, if not resolved, become issues. Role conflict can take the form of the classic model developed by Getzels (1958), where the personal needs of individuals conflict with the needs/ expectations of the organization. These conflicts arise in numerous and varied ways. For example, the school may expect a teacher to work with others in a group or team-teach, while the teacher prefers to work alone. Conflict usually occurs when individuals believe that another is acting outside of his/her role or not fulfilling the expectations of the role. One might hear "He is not supposed to do that" or "She is not doing her job." It is imperative that the leader and followers have a mutual understanding of the expectations of the various roles within the school/district. Both job descriptions and performance evaluations must be aligned and conform to the agreed-upon expectations of the particular role.

Issue resolution is another competency essential to leadership. Issues develop out of differing opinions or beliefs on a host of topics, such as policy, practice, goals, the means for reaching goals, values, etc. The wise leader welcomes issues and views them as an opportunity for improvement and better understanding of all parties. As with role conflict, problem-solving approaches work best. Typically, the leader seeks consensus on the goals of either side of an issue and ensures both sides fully understand the opposing position. The leader then solicits all concerns and attempts to find a different and better solution that either side proposes. In this manner, when one side is in favor of Plan A and their opposing side is either in favor of Plan B or simply against Plan A, the leader seeks a Plan C. Future leaders must utilize research, practice, reflect, and form habits of resolving conflict and issues.

Analysis Questions for Conflict and Issue Resolution
To what extent:

♦ Do all persons within the organization understand the duties and responsibilities of his or her position and the positions of others?
♦ Are expectations for others realistic and aligned with job descriptions?
♦ Is conflict seen as an opportunity?
♦ Have steps been taken to resolve personal conflict and/or issue conflict?
♦ Have steps moved both sides toward a different and better solution?

What actions need to be taken to address any concerns from above to solve the current problem and avoid similar problems in the future?

6. Motivating and Developing Others
No human venture succeeds without strongly motivated men and women (Gardner, 1990). The wise leader understands that there is no universal motivation for every individual, but seeks to discover what motivates the people that he/she leads. There are many theories on motivation and each may be partly true for some people.

There is a deep tradition of behavioral thinking in public schools. For all practical purposes, behavioral theories are not accepted or used by most psychologists. The field has moved past Pavlov and Skinner, who believed that the key to increasing motivation is to provide consistent and appropriate consequences to reinforce desired behaviors. Alfie Kohn challenged the reliance on rewards to motivate individuals with his provocative 1993 book *Punished by Rewards*. He contends that hundreds of studies have shown that rewards produce only temporary compliance and that no lasting change in attitudes or behaviors can be attributed to the use of rewards. Control over others and the manipulation of reality is inappropriate and unethical. Unfortunately, many school leaders wonder, "What rewards and punishments can we use to induce others to act appropriately?" Leaders need to move from behavioral perspectives to cognitive motivation and learning theory and practice.

The intern must be knowledgeable of motivation theory and attempt to increase motivation for improvement. The key is to understand what motivates (or inspires) each member of the organization. Future leaders must utilize research, practice, reflect, and form habits of motivating everyone they lead.

Analysis Questions for Motivation
To what extent:

♦ Are the needs of the people being met?
♦ Are the needs of the people in line with the needs or the organization?
♦ Are differing processes used to motivate? Are they effective?
♦ Are varying methods used to develop others?

What actions need to be taken to address any concerns from above to solve the current problem and avoid similar problems in the future?

7. Managing Group Processes
Warren Bennis (2000) believes that our world is the product of "Great Groups," teams of creative persons who banded together to achieve remarkable successes that would not have been possible through a traditional hierarchical approach. The traditional school, however, is a place where work is done individually.

Breaking with this tradition and reforming the culture where faculty and administrators collaboratively work toward school improvement requires commitment to empowerment, developing new leaders, cooperation, and shared responsibility. Leaders must invest time, effort, and expertise to overcome traditions, past failures, and lack of interest and/ or expertise on the part of faculty (and administrators) to work together. Overcoming prior negative attitudes is a difficult, but not impossible, task. It is the responsibility of the leader to provide new positive experiences in working in groups with shared goals, shared responsibility, shared authority, and shared decision-making.

Calling in the entire faculty to announce what could have been put in writing is insulting and a waste of time. Likewise, calling a meeting to discuss failures of a few faculty wastes the time of all others. The need to meet should be common sense. Meeting involves discussion, learning, group thinking, and group work. Obviously, a leader should develop a set of principles or rules for meetings and use effective skills in conducting the meeting.

The following is an example of rules for meetings:

♦ Schedule meetings only when necessary and there is a need to meet. Information that can be put in writing should be communicated through email, memos, or other means of two-way communication between meetings.
♦ Prior to the meeting, distribute an agenda with purpose, time, and location listed. Participants in meetings should come prepared and know that they have a say in their meetings and that their input is valued.
♦ Meetings should be arranged and organized for participation. The leader may use a circle or semi-circle or at least stand or sit on the same level.
♦ The leader should solicit participation from and show interest in individual members. He/she should model listening skills and value the comments and conflicting perspectives from the members.
♦ The leader should stay on time and on task. Often, leaders plan for more than can be accomplished at one meeting. Thus, time management is vital and the leader is responsible for keeping to the item or task at hand.
♦ The leader summarizes accomplishments of the meeting and follows up on decisions. Followers quickly lose respect and trust in leaders that speak well but do not follow up. Followers expect meetings to produce results. Follow-up is crucial in establishing a culture where meetings are viewed as important and productive.

Faculty members meet at other times than in leader-called meetings. This may be grade-level or subject-area department meetings, committees, task forces, or a host of other types of groups. If the leader expects these meetings to be productive, training must be given. Members need guidelines, adequate information, clear understanding of purposes and goals, and to learn to work in a group. These groups may have an assigned leader, such as the department chair, or the task may be assigned and a leader may emerge. Productive groups do not just happen. They must be developed.

In order to overcome many negative attitudes of meetings, committees, and working groups, the leader must truly believe in others and their abilities to accomplish tasks and make effective decisions. It is imperative that future school leaders utilize research, practice, reflect, and form habits of effective group processes to solicit support, develop new leaders, and reach organizational goals.

Analysis Questions for Group Processes
To what extent:

♦ Have the formal and informal groups been identified?
♦ Are all groups working productively and collaboratively?
♦ Are goals for the groups realistic, understood, and acceptable?
♦ Is trust and freedom of expression the norm of all groups?
♦ Are meetings used effectively and efficiently?

What actions need to be taken to address any concerns from above to solve the current problem and avoid similar problems in the future?

8. Supporting Others With Appropriate Leadership Style
For decades, researchers have studied leadership style. They have coined many terms to describe leadership styles. Goleman (2000) devised six terms that describe various styles used by business leaders: coercive, commanding, affiliative, democratic, pacesetting, and coaching. He found coercive and pacesetting to be negative and the other four positive. For our purposes here, we will use the following six terms of styles to consider for appropriate use:

1. *Directive*. Similar to authoritative, autocratic, or commanding, this style is used when strict compliance is needed or it is an urgent/ emergency situation. The directive style is appropriate for quick changes or guidance. It is also appropriate when only the leader has the necessary knowledge or expertise.
2. *Participative*. Often labeled democratic, this style is used when limited time is available and/or the leader holds most of the accountability for the results. With this style, the leader makes the final decision or approves policy or practice, but gathers input from others. Ideally, this involves all those affected by the decision or action.
3. *Collaborative*. Also labeled democratic, this is the ideal style and is a means of working in true collaboration with others. This style values others' expertise and helps develop future leaders. This style requires adequate time, training, and a shared responsibility. In most cases, better decisions are made with the use of a collaborative style.
4. *Coaching*. The leader remains in a leader/teacher/mentor role with the subordinate. This is also an ideal style when followers are not prepared for true collaboration. Coaching frees the subordinate to practice as a leader, while remaining under the guidance and assistance of the formal leader.
5. *Affiliative*. This style is appropriate when the leader has more concern for the person or persons than the task. This could be when trying to build positive relationships or persons are dealing

with personal issues. Once the personal problem has passed or the relationship has been formed, the leader can focus on the task and use a coaching or collaborative style. It should be noted that this is opposite of Goleman's pacesetting style where the task takes precedence over people.

6. *Laissez-Faire.* This style is seldom recommended, but may be appropriate for minor tasks where followers have more expertise and interest than the leader.

The key to using the most effective style is to know the situation and people and strive to meet the needs of both. In some cases, the entire staff must be dealt with using a very directive style and at other times, only some of the staff needs a directive style. In some cases, some of the staff needs coaching, while others are at a level of collaboration. The main lesson is that people and situations, not the leader's preferences, dictate what style the leader should use.

Analysis Questions for Leadership Style

To what extent was the appropriate style used with differing people and/or in differing circumstances?

What actions need to be taken to address any concerns from above to solve the current problem and avoid similar problems in the future?

9. Using Power Ethically

A leader must wield power in order to accomplish great things. Although many believe power corrupts or no person should have power over another, power can be both positive and negative. The wise leader understands the negative potential of power but strives to use power for good. In the classic model of power, French and Raven (1959) believe there are five basic types of power: reward, coercive, legitimate, referent, and expert.

The use of *reward power* is tempting. Many believe it is right to reward others for their effort and feel a sense of joy in giving to those that deserve it. However, the use of reward power can do more harm than good. In giving rewards to some, others are overlooked. In giving rewards, some begin to expect it and may only work for reward or limit their efforts to the criteria set for the reward. Additionally, it is impossible to find a reward that everyone is willing to work for. The reward system becomes a "game" and many tire of playing. The end result is that the leader's power is diminished. Use of reward power is not recommended.

Coercive power is an obvious misuse of power. Yet, coercive power is often used with students. Making threats to children for misbehavior or poor academic performance carries over to administration, and threats are then made to faculty and staff. The use of coercive power is unethical. Coercion and punishment does not solve problems in schools. The wise leader refrains from using either reward or coercive power.

Legitimate power is derived from the authority given to the position. Superintendents have authority over principals; principals have authority over teachers; and teachers have authority over students. Depending on the history and culture of the district, however, the power given to a position may vary. Some teachers have very little power over students and some principals exert minimal power over the faculty. It is others that give power to the leader, so he/she cannot depend solely on the power of the position. The wise leader understands both the powers inherent to the position and the powers *not* given to the position.

Referent power is the ideal. Followers give power to leaders that they identify with, believe in, and trust. In order to increase referent power, the leader must know others and allow them to know him or her. The leader must work with others, find consensus in the vision, and determine the means of achieving the vision. Gaining referent power requires effective communication and a strong belief in the value of others and working together.

Expert power comes from possessing special knowledge or skill. Followers freely give power to experts for help and guidance. In order to increase expert power, the leader must commit time and effort to become more expert in essential areas of leadership and education.

The wise leader understands that empowering others in the quest for school improvement builds a broad power base. If one gives out power, he/she gains power. Only in politics would one view this as giving up power. Empowering others builds support, buy-in, consensus, and the development of current and future leaders. It is imperative that future school leaders utilize research, practice, reflect, and form habits of using appropriate style and power to reach organizational goals and positively and ethically meet the needs of everyone they lead.

Analysis Questions for Power
To what extent:

- Has the leader exerted the appropriate use of referent or expert power?
- Has the leader exerted the misuse of coercive or reward power?
- Is delegation of duties and power given in the organization?
- Do faculty, students, and parents feel empowered?

What actions need to be taken to address any concerns from above to solve the current problem and avoid similar problems in the future?

10. Creating and Managing a Positive Culture and Climate
The only thing of real importance that leaders do is to create and manage culture (Schein, 1992). This is best understood when one considers that the school's vision, ways of making decisions and communicating, amount and

type of conflict, degree of motivation, use of power, and the ability to change are all ingredients of the culture. The culture also includes the history, traditions, and beliefs of the organization, and the relative importance of each. People form attitudes toward the values, norms, expectations, and practices that set their school apart from others (Greenberg & Baron, 1997).

The leader is responsible for understanding the culture and promoting a more positive culture for all. He/she realizes that culture changes over time and that subcultures exist. Cultural changes need a shared commitment and require extensive follow-up for the change to become an accepted aspect of the new culture.

The leader should also be aware of the climate and take action if the current climate is negative in nature. School climate is simply defined as the feelings or atmosphere of the school. Climate can change quickly and often. The leader should be proactive in dealing with climate. The leader can use formal assessments, develop trusting relationships, have effective means for communicating, and seek to know the feelings and atmosphere on a daily basis. The leader should be very sensitive to and take responsibility for staff and student morale. He or she should investigate the causes for low morale and the steps that can be taken to raise morale.

Climate and culture are extremely important aspects for measuring the "quality of life" in the school. Quality of life affects academic performance, behavior, staff turnover, motivation, health, and the mental health of all members of the school. Future leaders must utilize research, practice, reflect, and form habits of assessing, improving, and creating a positive school culture and climate.

Analysis Questions for Culture and Climate
To what extent:

♦ Have adequate assessments been conducted to assess the culture and climate?
♦ Are there concerns with the current school culture or climate and, if so, have adequate time and resources been allocated for needed improvement?

What actions need to be taken to address any concerns from above to solve the current problem and avoid similar problems in the future?

11. Initiating Change
Successful leaders initiate and manage change. Of all of the skills presented in this text, leading change is the most difficult. Michael Fullan (2001b) asserts that there are two main aspects of educational change: what changes to implement (theories of education) and how to implement change (theories

of change). They interact and shape each other, but the critical factor is the distinctiveness of the individual setting. What works in one setting may not work in another.

What Do We Know About Change?

- It is a process that takes place over time (two to three years).
- The process has steps or stages and requires a change in belief.
- It must begin with the individual, and then out to the organization.
- It is difficult and seldom worth the effort, and most changes fail.
- A real need or pressure is required and not everyone will change.
- No amount of information will make the change totally clear.
- It will always have disagreement and conflict.
- The leader has a key role in facilitating.
- Those affected by change must be involved in the process.
- It must be evaluated and monitored from beginning to end.
- Improvement cannot occur without it.

The most startling aspect cited in the list above is that most change efforts fail. Most experts recommend attempting only one or two changes at a time. The wise leader must fully understand the change process and choose his/her change efforts wisely. Most people fear and/or resist change. Change causes disequilibrium in individuals and they seek the balance of the past.

What Are the Factors in Resistance to Change?

- Some agree with new programs but never do anything.
- Some need more time – they rationalize resistance.
- Some are against any change made from a state or national level.
- Some only rely on costs – is it worth the time and effort?
- Some only want incremental change and fear large change efforts.
- Some are successful and are very conservative toward change.
- Some lack the skill to make the change or have an honest difference of opinion.

Leaders can take appropriate actions to reduce resistance in spite of these factors. These include:

- Allow teachers to feel the change is their own.
- Show that the change reduces rather than increases their burdens.
- Involve others and reach consensus on the value of the change.
- Validate and recognize objections and give feedback and clarification.
- Develop support, trust, and confidence with those involved.

♦ Set attainable and realistic goals and be open to revision and improvement.
♦ Change and resistance to change are inevitable: the leader must guide and direct it.

Factors for successful change efforts:

♦ Broad-based ownership – including informal and formal power
♦ Positive relationships have been built
♦ Support from administration and community awareness
♦ Fits philosophy, mission, and culture of school
♦ Has a moral purpose and is relevant to those affected
♦ Planning, evaluation, and adequate resources are available
♦ Monitoring and adjustment in process occur
♦ More training occurs during implementation than at first
♦ Few, if any, other big changes are occurring at the same time

These lists were compiled from the works of Tony Wagner (1994), Robert Evans (1996), Gay Hendricks and Kate Ludeman (1996), Peter Senge et al. (1996), Hall and Hord (2001), and Michael Fullan (2002). It should be noted that the lack of any one variable might cause the change to fail.

It has been said that change is the only constant in life. It has also been said that everyone wants improvement, but no one wants change. The skill of effecting change is one that requires much thought, analysis, and effort. Despite the hurdles, if one is to lead, one must lead change. Future leaders must utilize research, practice, reflect, and form habits of leading educational change.

Analysis Questions for Change

To what extent:

♦ Is the change proposed only one of a few?
♦ Is there a moral purpose in the new change?
♦ Do all involved understand the change process?
♦ Have positive relationships been built?
♦ Is the creation and sharing of information a priority?
♦ Has a productive disturbance and a subsequent coherence been accomplished?
♦ Have steps been taken to reduce resistance?
♦ Have the factors that produce success been implemented?

What actions need to be taken to address any concerns from above to solve the current problem and avoid similar problems in the future?

12. Evaluating Student, Personnel, and Program Performance

The topic of evaluation is complex and controversial and involves many entities, subjects, criteria, and beliefs. The federal government, unions, accrediting agencies, boards of education, universities, real estate agencies, the press, and a host of professional organizations all rate and evaluate public schools. One might conclude that so many others get involved because we educators do a poor job of it.

If anything is worth doing, it is worth evaluating and finding improvements. Only through meaningful, valid, and reliable evaluation can strengths, weaknesses, conflicting efforts, and wasteful efforts emerge and allow leaders to analyze and take appropriate actions. Ratings and labeling do little to find answers. Evaluation must be thorough, having adequate breadth and depth.

Evaluations should be administered on the following:

♦ Faculty, staff, and students
♦ Recruiting, hiring, staff development, and retention
♦ Programs and co-curricular activities
♦ Curriculum, instruction, and testing
♦ Technology
♦ Community and parent relations
♦ Food service, transportation, facilities, and safety
♦ Fiscal accountability and legal compliance
♦ All 12 leadership competencies

This list is not exhaustive, but it does show the scope of what needs evaluation. Only through evaluative information can leaders plan appropriate action for improvement. The evaluation must begin with the existing practice and measure the extent of progress toward the vision or final goal. Beginning, formative, and summative measures should be taken at appropriate intervals. Care must be taken to choose evaluative instruments that reliably measure what you intend to measure.

The new bandwagon in educational leadership is data-driven decisions. Many new books are published to assist leaders in improving skills in collecting, analyzing, and using data for plans and decisions. It is highly recommended that future leaders study and develop new skills in the use of evaluative data to increase learning and the overall performance of the school.

Analysis Questions for Evaluation
To what extent:

♦ Are effective personnel and program evaluations established?
♦ Are both formative and summative evaluations utilized?
♦ Is data from evaluations used for decisions and planning?

What actions need to be taken to address any concerns from above to solve the current problem and avoid similar problems in the future?

Essential Competencies Activities

Review the sample case in Appendix G. At first reading, it seems to be a simple issue and requires a simple action. Notice that after analyzing the case, however, the leader found many aspects of his or her leadership in need of improvement. During the implementation of the internship plan, you will most probably encounter similar issues or concerns. Try to analyze the issue through addressing the analysis questions under each of the 12 essential competency areas above.

Choose one or two of the 12 competencies for which you want additional expertise. Review prior coursework, current research, and/or take part in additional training or interviews and devise a plan to better develop the competency. Focus on improving the competency over a period of time. Document your plan, goals, and activities and reflect on key learning. Following meeting your first competency development goals, choose another one or two competencies and repeat the process. Continue the process until all competencies needing additional practice and expertise have been addressed. Your plan, goals, and reflections will be included in the final internship report.

3.4 Journal

"The brain does its best reflective work when provided with the time, place, and tools for the deliberate exercise of reasoning skills" (Dickmann & Stanford-Blair, 2002, p. 206). Benefits of journaling have been identified as expanding awareness, understanding, and insights; making connections between theory and practice; and generating new hypotheses for action (Taggart & Wilson, 2005). Interns should keep a reflective journal of their building-level internship experiences, as a companion to their logs. Through these, interns can reflect on the significance of their internship activities for personal growth and achievement of school and district goals. The reflective journal is also a means for recording and examining practical and ethical dilemmas. The reflections should relate experiences to the professional standards.

Journaling assists the emerging leader in focusing on essential leadership skill, knowledge, and needed disposition. Journaling also provides an opportunity to reflect on results of the intern's efforts. The reflections should raise ideas about how an intern might alter or improve an activity as a school leader in the future and show evidence of reflective skills in application, analysis, synthesis, and evaluation. Time and thought used in journal writing reinforce the learning and assist in the leader's ability to truly begin reflection prior, during, and after action. Interns often keep journal entries in a separate file on the computer, while others prefer handwritten formats. The type of journal you keep is your choice, unless required otherwise by the university. You may find that journal entries help in compiling your final report.

Typical journal formats are:

♦ *Daily* (5–10 minutes) – Many try journaling daily for a two- to three-week period and then reflect on patterns found following this period.
♦ *Weekly* (30–45 minutes) – Many try journaling weekly for one month and then reflect on patterns found following this period.
♦ *Intermittent* – Many make journal entries following significant insights, feelings, and/or experiences.
♦ *Projects* – Many interns keep a journal while leading major projects and reflect on the leadership experience and results.

Guiding or key questions to assist in your reflective entries are:

♦ What are you learning about your leadership style, strengths, and/or development areas?
♦ What belief, experience, or disposition caused a particular judgment?
♦ Did you notice any personal feelings – e.g., stress, frustration, tired, or happy – warm relationships, etc.? What do you believe was the cause?
♦ How did you arrive at a decision made? Did you consider other alternatives? Why was your choice the best one?
♦ What are you learning about diversity (for example, but not limited to, race, culture, and language diversity, diversity of thought, diversity of educational approach)? Did you react differently to some students, peers, or supervisors than others? If so, why?
♦ What challenging leadership situations or leadership opportunities have you experienced and how have you addressed them?
  What did you learn and how might you address the situation or opportunity differently as a leader?
♦ What examples of best practice have you observed and how might you build upon those practices in your own leadership work?
♦ Did you observe any change in knowledge, skill, or disposition?
♦ How were your actions conducive to increased learning, school improvement, and/or development of self and others?
♦ How did your experience provide progress on mastery of state and/or national standards?

Reflection is an important learning strategy in leadership development. By stepping back and reflecting upon what was learned, what worked or did not work, and how course readings, experiences, and other theory and research might inform the work, candidates gain insight into understanding the nature of school and district leadership and their own leadership skill development and proficiency. Reflection with an advisor, supervisor, and peers is critical to one's self-development and is an essential practice for effective problem solving. It is recommended that an intern complete at least two journal entries per week. Reflective journals are submitted to the university-based internship supervisor, NOT to the school or district internship supervisor.

3.5 Log

The intern must meet with the supervisor and agree on the method of documenting the internship experience. Typically, logs should cite date, time (rounded to the half-hour), a brief statement describing the activity, and the state or national standard met. An example:

Date	Time	Description of Activity	Standard
9/05/16	1.0 hour	Conducted a classroom observation of Ms. Smith's history teaching.	8

Many internship programs require a reflective statement following each log entry. The advantage to this is that interns must reflect immediately following the entry into the log. Other programs separate the journal and summative log with a requirement of a more in-depth reflective journal entry. The intern should meet with the supervisor and collaboratively decide on the method that best meets the needs of the intern and program.

3.6 Organizing a Portfolio

The intern is required to obtain and use a document portfolio or e-portfolio. Universities differ in the kinds of programs they use for the e-portfolio. You will need to check with your university supervisor for that information. Interns may organize their portfolios with sections devoted to the 52 skill and experience areas. Some students organize with the national and/ or state standards. Again, consult with your university supervisor for requirements for organization of the portfolio. Keep in mind that leaders keep a professional portfolio during their career. It will be your choice whether you decide to use a document portfolio or electronic portfolio following your internship. Following certification and administrative experience, the portfolio is typically reorganized with sections of administrative duties or positions.

3.7 Monitoring/Formative Evaluation

Plans always have to be changed. Typically, these changes occur as a result of:

♦ Unexpected events
♦ New opportunities

- ♦ Suggestions/recommendations from mentors and/or interviewees
- ♦ New perspectives gained from experience and reflection
- ♦ Results of periodic formative evaluations

Any or all of the above can arise and cause the intern to adjust, add, and/or delete planned activities. The intern should determine and schedule periodic assessment of their progress and plan. Formative evaluation should be completed monthly or more often, if needed. This should be a combination of self-evaluation and supervisor observation. It is recommended that after self-evaluation on progress and accomplishments, the intern meet with his/her supervisor and collaboratively discuss the quality and quantity of intern activities undertaken thus far and timelines for completing the remainder of planned activities. The discussion should include gains in knowledge, skill, disposition, and effects on learning and school improvement. The formative evaluations should note any changes to the plan. Changes should have a brief explanation of the circumstances and rationale for the change.

Summative Evaluation/ Final Report

In this final activity, the intern will prepare and present the concluding summative report. Typically, the intern will present to his/her supervisors, either as part of many reports by others or individually. The report should be a professional presentation, similar to reporting to the board. Documentation should include the items listed below. University requirements may vary so be certain to check with your supervisor.

4.1 Internship/Practicum Log

The completed log must be submitted in accordance to your program requirements. The log should include, but not be limited to, the following:

- ◆ Beginning and ending dates of the internship
- ◆ Total number of hours and approximate percentages of hours observing, participating, and leading
- ◆ Brief description of activities and dates performed
- ◆ Name and title of school site mentor/supervisor and contact information

4.2 Professional Standards Assessment/Progress

The intern must complete a summary and evaluation of experience for *each* of the ten NPBEA professional standards. One summary and evaluation for each area is required, regardless of the amount of time or number of activities accomplished in the particular leadership standard. The summary and evaluation of each standard should be approximately one page and include the following:

- ◆ Overview/summary of activities performed for the standard
- ◆ Key learnings from the experience (knowledge, skill, and/or disposition)
- ◆ Area(s) needing further experience and improvement
- ◆ Personal assessment of the degree of mastery of the standard

4.3 Impact on Student Learning and/or Learning Environment

The intern must demonstrate how he/she was able to increase student learning and/or improve the learning environment during the internship. Review the logs and reflective journal and cite examples of actions taken that demonstrate increased student learning and/or an improved learning environment. If an action research project was conducted, it should be included in this section.

4.4 Dispositions and Interpersonal Skill Assessment/Progress

The intern should briefly describe the dispositions and interpersonal skills that they focused upon during the internship and provide evidence (new beliefs, feelings, actions taken, etc.) that shows a positive change in the disposition or skill. Also, include dispositions and interpersonal skills that need further development and how you plan to address these needs.

4.5 Reflective Practice

Competence grows as one observes more. The goal was to observe more and have a greater range of models to draw from as you reflected on your own actions and the actions of others. The intern will summarize and provide highlights of his/her experience with reflective practice. Also include an overall *reflection on practice* discussing the following:

- ♦ What models/concepts/theories were effective or not effective?
- ♦ What deep-seated beliefs guided your actions and experience?
- ♦ How did the history/traditions/culture of the district/school affect your actions?
- ♦ How did your emotional state/moods affect your actions and experience?
- ♦ How did the availability or lack of resources affect your actions?
- ♦ How did the on-the-job experience change your beliefs and actions?
- ♦ How and in what ways have you been prepared for school leadership? In what areas have you experienced leadership growth and development the most? Where is further development critical?
- ♦ How have your instructional leadership skills improved since you began the program? What internship experiences contributed to this development and improvement?
- ♦ How has your understanding of the role of leadership to foster social justice and promote equity changed throughout the program?

How has your internship contributed to your understanding? What leadership skills have you developed to support this role?

♦ In what ways did you contribute to school improvement through your internship? What leadership skills and practices did you use? What challenges did you experience and what have you learned for your future work as a school leader?

♦ How has your commitment to a career in school leadership changed through the internship and what are your current goals?

4.6 Action Research/Project Leadership

If an action research study was conducted, the intern will submit an Action Research Report including the following:

♦ Background of study (school demographics, problem addressed, research question)
♦ Review of the literature or benchmark information
♦ Methodology (intervention, population/sample, data collection used)
♦ Findings
♦ Conclusions and Recommendations from the study
♦ Lessons learned from leading the study

If an action research project was not conducted, the intern will submit a report of the project or projects that he/she led. The report should include:

♦ Description of the project
♦ Goals of the project
♦ Results/Findings from the project
♦ Lessons learned from leading the project

4.7 Essential Competencies Development

The intern will include a brief (1/2 to 1 page each) description of any of the 12 essential competencies that he/she focused upon during the internship. Cite examples of activities or experiences that were undertaken. Briefly describe the learning from the activity or experience.

4.8 Ethical and Critical Reasoning

The intern will include a summary description of activities undertaken in regard to ethical and critical reasoning. Note key learnings from the experience and recommendations for better ethical practice in the schools.

4.9 Social Justice

The intern will briefly describe the degree of social justice that he/she encountered in the school/district. Cite actions taken during the internship that promoted an increase in social justice. Include recommendations for school policy and practice to better address social justice.

4.10 New Technologies

The intern will briefly describe experience and key learning in the areas of administrative technology and technology for learning. Include areas needing further experience and training.

4.11 Future Professional Development Plan

The intern must prepare and submit a three-year professional development plan based on his or her internship experience. Typically, a professional development plan focuses on the priorities or greatest needs of the leader. The plan must be clear, manageable, and include a means of evaluation.

A clear plan lists specific objectives. These may include particular skill development, reevaluating dispositions, or attaining new knowledge, etc. It should cite actions to be taken, as opposed to a vague or general intent to improve in a particular area. This could include additional courses, workshops, books, working with a mentor, or a host of other experiences. The intern should research available resources to meet his/her objectives. Exact titles or dates of future training may not be available at this time.

A plan that is manageable includes actions that can be accomplished in a reasonable amount of time. Typically, three to five objectives are included in a three-year plan. This allows the intern time to use or practice the new knowledge, disposition, or skill. A timeline for each objective must be included. The plan must cite the criteria used to judge whether the objective was met. Ideally, this would be an artifact or other evidence that could be included in the portfolio.

4.12 Developing the Portfolio

A portfolio is a compilation of relevant *evidence* of your knowledge, skill, and disposition. It may include degrees and certificates, but is primarily the best samples of your professional work and accomplishments. A professional portfolio should not be a scrapbook of training certificates, school papers, or notes from students.

Secondary principal interns should review the state, NPBEA, and NASSP standards. Elementary principal interns should review the state, NPBEA, and NAESP standards. It is recommended that you use one of these as your portfolio sections and provide *evidence* that you meet or are progressing in meeting these standards.

At this point in your leadership development, it is understood that you may not have documentation or evidence of meeting all the standards. This is the beginning of your portfolio, however, and should serve to guide the planning of future professional development. Submit the portfolio or link to the e-portfolio. Check with the university supervisor for specific requirements.

4.13 Vita Update

The intern should update his/her vita to include relevant accomplishments from the internship. This may be included in the leadership section of the vita for those not currently holding an administrative position. Guidelines for developing the vita are listed in Appendix A. A copy of the updated vita should be presented in the final internship report.

4.14 Letter of Application

The letter of application should focus on the specific career goal of the intern. For example, if the intern wants the position of curriculum or athletic director, the letter of application should be written for that position. If the intern would like an assistant principal position prior to applying for a principalship, the letter should be written for that position. Guidelines for the letter of application are listed in Appendix B. The letter of application should be presented in the final internship report.

4.15 School Improvement Recommendations

An intern has a unique perspective on school leadership. From your perspective, develop a prioritized list of recommendations for overall school improvement. The list may include recommendations for leaders, teachers, staff, parents, and/or community members. The list may also include recommendations for curriculum, instructions, assessment, discipline, or any other areas you believe can be improved and lead to greater student learning and satisfaction with the school experience. The list will be submitted as part of the internship final report.

Appendices

■ Appendix A   Sample Vita and Guidelines

George Washington
1508 West 14th Street, Mt Vernon, AZ 50555
(W) (303) 555-7837; (H) (303) 555-9069; gwash@used.org

Education/Certification

M.Ed.	Educational Leadership, Northern Arizona University, Flagstaff, AZ, 2014
B.A.	English, Carleton College, Northfield, MN, 1993
Principal Certificate	Arizona (In progress)
Teacher Certificate	7–12 English, Arizona and Minnesota
ESL Education	K–12 Endorsement, Arizona and Minnesota

Administrative and Leadership Experience

Assistant Principal, Martha High School, Mt. Vernon Union High School District, Vernon, AZ, 2000–present.

Administered campus activities including over 50 school clubs, school facility use, and school ceremonies.

Expanded the student recognition program designed to reward and promote student attendance, academic achievement, and responsible actions on campus.

Evaluated and provided guidance for a variety of teachers throughout the school using the district's evaluation instrument and informal observations and conferences.

English Department Chairperson, Martha High School, Mt. Vernon, AZ, 1999–2000.

Designed a department-based professional literacy library and conference center to help teachers better their pedagogical skills.

Implemented an English department collaborative teaching plan that promoted positive teacher communication regarding units and lessons, methodology, classroom management, and student achievement.

Planned and presented various English department in-services designed to improve classroom instruction, time management, and grant writing.

Evaluated all English teachers using the district's evaluation instrument and informal observations while carefully monitoring the progress of new and inexperienced teachers.

North Central Accreditation Writing Goal Chairman, Martha High School, Mt. Vernon, AZ, 1999–present.

Designed and implemented an in-service program for teachers in all subject areas to ensure successful writing instruction across the curriculum.

Presented instructional methodology to assist all staff members in teaching and using the six-trait writing rubric, creating quality writing prompts, and paragraph and essay organization.

Learning 24/7 Leadership Team Member, Martha High School, Mt. Vernon, AZ 2000–present.

Advised and designed a school-wide plan to assure our students' success in the classroom, on standardized tests, and in life.

Aligned school curricula, incorporated test-taking skills into the curriculum, created a strong school-wide emphasis on basic reading, writing, and math skills in every class, and incorporated critical thinking skills across the curriculum.

Evaluated the specific instructional needs of our students and teachers by meticulously surveying and analyzing student test data, grades, and district assessments.

Head Basketball Coach, Martha High School, Mt. Vernon, AZ, 1995–2000.

Incorporated a successful parent booster club that raised funds to support the basketball program.

Created a successful basketball program that won at least 19 games in each of the last three seasons while maintaining a team grade point average greater than a 3.2.

Teaching Experience

High School English Teacher – Martha High School, Mt. Vernon, AZ, 1994–2000.

Integrated a variety of teaching methods and instructional strategies to generate student interest.

Evaluated and tracked student progress in class by using a combination of evaluations and student work samples.

Maintained positive relationship with students and parents while holding students to a high standard of acceptable class work.

Upward Bound English Teacher – Normandale Upward Bound Program, Normandale Community College, Richfield, MN, 1994.

Designed a writing workshop for students involved to create, edit, and revise their own work in a summer writing portfolio.

Published a variety of works from every student's summer writing portfolio in a book distributed to all students and parents at the end of the summer.

Coaching Experience

Head Basketball Coach, Martha High School, Mt. Vernon, AZ, 1995–2000.

Incorporated a successful parent booster club that raised funds to support the basketball program.

Created a successful basketball program that won at least 19 games in each of the last three seasons while maintaining a team grade point average greater than a 3.2.

Additional Training/Professional Development

"Cutting Edge Grant Writing," Otter Creek Institute, Phoenix, AZ, May 2000.

"Increasing Student Achievement," National School Conference Institute, Phoenix, AZ, March 2000.

Presentations

Washington, G. (2000, September). *Improving Student Writing.* Presentation at the Inter-District Articulation Program, Mt. Vernon, AZ.

Washington, G. (2000, September). *Incorporating Writing in All Classrooms.* Presentation at the Martha High School Faculty In-service, Mt. Vernon, AZ.

Washington, G. (2000, August). *NCA Writing Goal and the Six-Trait Writing Rubric.* Presentation at the Martha High School In-service Program, Mt. Vernon, AZ.

Professional Affiliations

Association for Supervision and Curriculum Development, 1999–present

National Association of Secondary School Principals, 2000–present

Arizona Professional Educators, 2000–present

Reference

References will be included on the following page, if requested.

Guidelines for the Development of the Vita

Overall Guidelines

1) Well-defined categories/sections in appropriate order
2) Neat and conservative (on white or beige, more space than type)
3) Accurate and Ethical
4) Accomplishment oriented
5) Results of accomplishments shown, if any (supportive evidence in portfolio)
6) Information outside of professional life omitted
7) Clear, readable font (size 12 for most fonts)
8) Grammatically correct (consistent use of past tense verbs)
9) Several pages in length (not the one-page business resume)

Preferred Order of Categories

Choose the categories that are most accurate, ethical, and appropriate. Other categories or combinations of these and others for unique individuals and/or experiences may be used.

Heading
Education/Certification
Administrative, Supervisory, and/or Leadership Experience
Teaching Experience
Coaching Experience (if applicable)
Related Experience (if applicable)
Other Experience (if applicable)
Professional Development
Publications and/or Presentations and/or Grants (if applicable)
Curriculum Experience (if applicable)
Professional Affiliations
Honors and/or Awards (if applicable)
Community Involvement/Service
Professional References
Reference Page

Heading Guidelines

a) Heading should be three lines in length
b) Name should **stand out** and be legal name
c) Provide complete address, phone number(s) with area codes, and e-mail address

Education/Certification Category Guidelines

a) Degree should be highlighted
b) Following degree is area of degree, institution, city, state, and year awarded

c) Major and/or minor may be listed, if appropriate and useful
d) Address of institution is not needed
e) Note any significant amount of hours taken, not leading to degree
f) Skip one line to separate certificates from degrees
g) Certificates are cited exactly as written on certificate and include state
h) List administrative certificate(s) first
i) Place any endorsements after teaching certificates
j) Include current certification sought – use (In progress) or (Expected completion date, [month and year])

Administrative and/or Leadership Category Guidelines

a) Use Administrative Experience category only if you were certified and served in an administrative position. It is unethical to invent a title, i.e., Assistant Principal, if you only assisted the Principal.
b) Use Supervisory Experience category only if you were certified and served in a supervisory position (supervising adults).
c) Use Leadership Experience category for all other leadership roles, i.e., Department or Grade Level Chair, Committee Chair, Site Council Member, etc.
d) Categories are combinable, for example, Supervisory/Leadership Experience, if experience in both.
e) List title first, then school, city, state, and date(s).
f) Use bullets and relevant past tense verbs for all accomplishments, for example, wrote, implemented, supervised, etc.
g) List any results of accomplishment, if known and appropriate.
h) Use two to six bullets under each title.

Teaching Experience Category Guidelines

a) Capitalize and list title first, then organization or school, city, state, and date(s)
b) Use bullets and relevant past tense verbs, for example, wrote, implemented, supervised, etc.
c) List any results of accomplishment, if known
d) Use two to six bullets, typically more if very recent or significant number of years in the following format:

Title, organization or school, city, state, date(s)

♦ Past tense verb + accomplishment + results
♦ Past tense verb + accomplishment + results
♦ Past tense verb + accomplishment
♦ Past tense verb + accomplishment

Coaching, Related, and/or Other Experience Category Guidelines

a) Use same format as above under Teaching Experience guidelines
b) Use Coaching Experience category if duty was contracted and experience was significant. List minor coaching duties as bullet(s) under Teaching Experience category
c) Use Related Experience category if duties are related to teaching/administrative duties
d) Use Other Experience category if significant experience, e.g., former career, etc.

Professional Development Category Guidelines

a) Cite the title first, then organization, city, state, and date(s)
b) There is no limit to the number of citations in this category
c) All training cited should be relevant to education/leadership
d) Note number of hours (if a significant amount)

Presentations and/or Publications Category Guidelines

a) Cite all presentations and/or publications in APA or other appropriate format
b) For five or fewer citations, use combination of categories – Presentations/Publications. If more than five and at least two in each, use separate Presentation and Publication categories
c) Be sure to include all co-authors or co-presenters
d) Consider citing dissertations, theses, and locally published curricular materials

Professional Affiliations Category Guidelines

a) Cite all current memberships in professional organizations
b) Note any offices held
c) Cite membership in any professional organizations of significant duration
d) Spell out complete names of organizations – do not use acronyms

Honors/Awards/Scholarship Category Guidelines

a) Use relevant category if you have two or more citations – otherwise, list under Teaching or Administrative category
b) Use combination of categories, if appropriate
c) Cite Honor, Award, or Scholarship, then organization, city, state, and date

Civic/Community Service Category Guidelines

a) List title, organization, city, state, and date(s)
b) Service should be related to goals or duties of the education profession instead of purely personal

c) Service to a particular church or religion may be used or if viewed as personal information, should not be cited

References Category Guidelines
a) Use as last category on vita
b) It is unethical to include references with vita, unless references requested
c) Be sure references gave permission to use their names

References Page Guidelines
a) List name and title first
b) List name of school or organization next
c) List complete address, city, state, and zip code
d) List phone number with area code and email address
e) This *must* be a separate page
f) Cite no more than six references
g) Must have reference for each place worked – if more than six, stay within last 10 years
h) Try to use administrator references – personal references are not appropriate
i) Cite references in order of priority – often only the first three are contacted

Sample reference page listing:
Dr. Bill Hickok, Principal
Page Elementary
184 Avenue C
Tombstone, AZ 85365
(520) 783–9999; bh@isp.edu

Frequently Asked Questions

Q: Shouldn't the vita be organized by years and have them in the left margin?

A: No. That is a style used for a business resume, not an educational vita.

Q: Should I use expensive paper with bright colors to make it stand out?

A: Neither expensive nor inexpensive paper is necessary, but you may use a good quality paper. Brightly colored paper is a tactic used in the world of business. Your experience and accomplishments should stand out, not the color of the paper.

Q: What if I have gaps of time in my vita?

A: You should exercise good judgment in this case. Often those with gaps in their career are raising children or tending to a sick family member or any other reasonable use of their time. There are others, however, that were fired and could not get another job, were in drug rehabilitation, or any other very personal reason. The point is that the reviewer of your vita may have doubts about which group you are in. Thus, unless your reasons are extremely personal, it is recommended that you provide some explanation for gaps in time to prevent the doubts of prospective employers.

Q: I do not have much in the leadership category. Should I list "leading students" in various activities or groups?

A: Your inexperience with leadership should motivate you to volunteer or apply for positions that will give you the necessary experience. Do not wait for an administrative position in order to gain leadership experience. There are many committees to chair, councils to serve on, and programs to lead while still teaching. Use your vita as a learning experience and start filling in the gaps.

Q: What if my coaching experience is quite extensive?

A: This is another judgment call. Much will depend on the position you are applying for. If, for example, you are applying for an Assistant Principal/Athletic Director position, then a complete listing of your coaching experience would be appropriate. If you were applying for solely an Assistant Principal position, then you would limit your coaching experience category and use as much as appropriate in the leadership experience category. Many duties and responsibilities in athletics leadership are the same as in school administration.

Q: What if I do not belong to any professional organizations?

A: It's time to join! Choose what is appropriate to your career goals. High school and middle school level principals may join the National Association of Secondary School Administrators (NASSP), elementary principals may join the National Association of Elementary Principals (NAESP), and those interested in curriculum development may join the Association for Supervision and Curriculum Development (ASCD). It is recommended that you also become active in the state affiliations for these professional organizations and read their journals regularly. Again, you do not have to wait to get the position to learn more about the position.

Q: What if I do not have any awards or honors?

A: Many great educators never received any honors or awards. Others were honored or recognized after their career ended. Honors and awards are bestowed on you by others – do not seek awards or honors, but graciously accept them.

Q: Should I or shouldn't I list church activities?

A: In public education, we are bound by separation of church and state. While active involvement with a particular church may denote many positive aspects of your service and character, it may also be viewed by some as interfering with the goals of public education. This is another judgment you must make.

With your vita, letter of application, and interview, your responsibility is to clearly show the prospective school district who you are. This is your half of the work leading up to the contract. If a religious affiliation is such a big part of you that it goes with you into school, then it would be appropriate to cite your church work. If your religious affiliation is more personal in nature and is not brought into the school, then omitting it from your professional vita would be appropriate.

Q: Why must the reference page be separate?

A: Persons willing to provide reference information for you are assuming districts very interested in hiring you will contact them. They should not have to provide information to every district where you applied. Therefore, it is considered unethical to provide references, unless requested in the job announcement or by the employer.

Q: Why list accomplishments?

A: Leaders accomplish things! This includes all educational leaders, especially teachers. A vita that shows only where and when you worked does not give any indication of accomplishment. Did you simply show up every day, or did you set goals and accomplish them? Accomplishment-oriented vitae do a much better job of showing who the leaders are. You should spend time analyzing your accomplishments (often forgotten or taken for granted) and list under the appropriate position.

Q: Is the vita changeable?

A: Although one cannot change the facts, one can add facts and/or present them differently. One designs the vita according to the position sought. For example, the district may desire curricular experience for the position. In this case, an applicant could include a Curriculum Experience category and place it higher up in the list of categories used. Another example is a district that wants primary experience. In this case, the intern adds her student teaching to the vita (normally not included) because that was her only primary experience. In short, you should try to match your vita with the position.

Appendix B

Sample Letter of Application and Guidelines

Sara Teacher
555 Maple Avenue
Miami, FL 50001
(999) 555–2122

April 15, 2014

Jack Armstrong, Personnel Director
ABC School District
Ft. Lauderdale, FL 50000

This letter is to officially apply for the position of Assistant Principal at Baywatch Elementary School. I am fully aware of the duties and responsibilities of the position. My education, teaching experience, and certification meet all of the posted requirements. After serious consideration, colleague support, and our administration advising that I apply, I am certain that I am ready and prepared to assume the duties of the Assistant Principal.

I bring to the position twelve years of successful teaching. This includes four years working with minority and poverty students, two years with gifted and talented, and eight years with numerous inclusive special education students. My students have performed better than the district and state average on tests and very few have needed administrative disciplinary assistance. I have formed excellent relationships with parents and members of the community. My successful teaching performance has allowed me to serve in many leadership capacities. I have served as grade-level Chair, Site Council representative, textbook committee Chair, math curriculum Chair, and sponsored numerous student organizations and school programs.

My administrative internship allowed me to gain experience in teacher observations, student discipline, budgeting and purchasing, staff development, and general office duties and responsibilities. I have taken an active part in special education reviews, expulsion hearings, hiring interviews, parent conferences, and the opening and ending school-year procedures. I understand the duties and operations of pupil and staff personnel, federal programs, transportation, athletics, and the curriculum department. I fully understand the role of the Assistant Principal and how to fulfill the needs of the various departments listed above.

I believe strongly in collaboration. This includes both the Principal and administrative staff and the faculty and students. I believe better decisions are made through participation and effective communication. I believe our first priority is student learning, whether academic or social. I believe in modeling fairness, openness, and honesty and always acting in an ethical manner. I believe what we do has a much greater impact on others than what we say. I believe in the goodness of everyone and that care and concern for others is the first step to reaching them and finding ways for them to achieve success.

I believe my knowledge, skill, and experience can greatly assist the ABC District in meeting its vision, mission, and goals. I know I will assist teachers in planning and implementing lessons, remediation, and effective evaluation techniques. I will provide the support and leadership that the teachers and staff expect and desire. I will treat them with the respect and professionalism that they deserve. I will continue to set high expectations for the faculty, the students, and myself. Although my main focus is on support, motivation, and preventative strategies, I am very firm with any individuals that are not meeting expectations. I will demand excellence, but will make all efforts to coach and assist them to reach excellence.

I have thoroughly enjoyed teaching and look forward to offering my experience, dedication, and skills to the faculty of Baywatch Elementary. I look forward to learning from and working with the current Principal and fellow administrators. I appreciate your review of my letter, application, vita, and supporting documents. I look forward to discussing my role as Assistant Principal with you further. If any additional information is needed, please advise.

Respectfully,

Sara Teacher

Guidelines for the Letter of Application

In drafting the letter, the intern must assess his/her knowledge, disposition, skill, and the match to the position and district. The letter of application will be the first impression you make of your career plans, experiences, and how you may benefit the district. It should bring out the highlights of your vita and your knowledge of the district and position. It is an opportunity to explain and expand your vita with a sample of your writing, philosophy, and vision and how these conform to the needs and expectations of the district/ school. The letter of application should have the following four sections:

Section 1 – Intent of Letter

The first paragraph must begin with the purpose or intent of the letter. In this case, you should write that you are officially applying for the particular position. Next, you should include that you are aware of the duties and responsibilities of the position. (If you are not currently knowledgeable of this position, be sure to acquire this knowledge during your internship experience.) Next, you should include a statement as to whether you meet all of the qualifications. If you do not, you should either specify which qualifications you do not meet or indicate how or when they will be met.

Some applicants include a personal bit of information in this section. This could be that you are excited about the possibility of assuming this position or that you have been preparing for this position, or whatever. If you decide to add a personal statement, be sure that it is honest and relevant.

Section 2 – Your Half of the Match

This section includes the highlights of the knowledge, skill, and experience that you are bringing to the district. This is your offer to the district. This is what they will be getting. It is written with the intent of informing the district what you can offer them for the future versus what you accomplished for someone else in the past. An example of this is to state that you bring two years of experience in administering a primary reading program, instead of stating that you ran the Distar Program for the XYZ District. Although this is a subtle distinction, keep in mind that districts are looking for someone to belong and work for them, not an outsider.

This section is an opportunity to summarize your vita. For example, you can include the highest degree attained, total number of years in education, relevant training or experience, etc. You can also provide further explanation and/or additional information not included in your vita. Examples could include your background, types of students you have worked with, evaluations, successes with particular students, or other relevant information.

This section should also include your principles, beliefs, philosophy, and vision. The intent here is to provide a deeper understanding of your character and your style. Again, it needs to be future-oriented and relate to how you will demonstrate these qualities in your new position. Much time and thought should be used in preparing this section. Consider the key beliefs and the guiding principles that you will rely on in your new leadership position.

Section 3 – Your Match With the District

Ideally, this section shows how your knowledge, skill, and experience meet the current and future needs of the district. This will require that you become knowledgeable of the history, current issues, and future demands of the district. The intern must do the work of gathering information about the district/school and the particular position sought. You must analyze the needs of the district and position, in light of your experience and abilities. This is your opportunity to show that you are the right match.

Section 4 – Thankful and Bold Conclusion

This section concludes your letter of application. It should offer a thank you for the time and effort the district took to review your application materials. It should also make a bold statement of your expectation of being hired or continuing in the hiring process. An example of this is to state that you look forward to the further discussion of your accepting this position. This is much more positive and bold than concluding with a hope of hearing from them. If you have accurately assessed yourself and the district and know that you will be successful in meeting the needs of the position, you deserve to be bold. As with the first paragraph of the letter of application, you may choose to add any other personal or relevant items to this section. Use your best judgment.

Application Letter Guidelines

- ♦ One to one-and-a-half pages in length
- ♦ Short, clear paragraphs
- ♦ Describes you, not your previous employer
- ♦ Outlines the realization of the district's goals, not your own
- ♦ Shows you have done your homework (know district/school and their needs)
- ♦ Is checked and rechecked – grammar, spelling, style, intent
- ♦ Is positive and void of anything negative (Districts want positive leadership)
- ♦ Clearly describes YOU and gives the district the opportunity to assess the match between you and the position

**National Policy Board for
Educational Administration
Professional Standards for
Educational Leaders 2015**

Standard One: Mission, Vision, and Core Values

Effective educational leaders develop, advocate, and enact a shared mission, vision, and core values of high-quality education and academic success and well-being of each student. Effective Leaders:

a) Develop an educational mission for the school to promote the academic success and well-being of each student.

b) In collaboration with members of the school and the community and using relevant data, develop and promote a vision for the school on the successful learning and development of each child and on instructional and organizational practices that promote such success.

c) Articulate, advocate, and cultivate core values that define the school's culture and stress the imperative of child-centered education; high expectations and student support; equity, inclusiveness, and social justice; openness, caring, and trust; and continuous improvement.

d) Strategically develop, implement, and evaluate actions to achieve the vision for the school.

e) Review the school's mission and vision and adjust them to changing expectations and opportunities for the school, and changing needs and situations of students.

f) Develop shared understanding of and commitment to mission, vision, and core values within the school and the community.

g) Model and pursue the school's mission, vision, and core values in all aspects of leadership.

Standard Two: Ethics and Professional Norms

Effective educational leaders act ethically and according to professional norms to promote each student's academic success and well-being. Effective Leaders:

a) Act ethically and professionally in personal conduct, relationships with others, decision-making, stewardship of the school's resources, and all aspects of school leadership.

b) Act according to and promote the professional norms of integrity, fairness, transparency, trust, collaboration, perseverance, learning, and continuous improvement.

c) Place children at the center of education and accept responsibility for each student's academic success and well-being.

d) Safeguard and promote the values of democracy, individual freedom and responsibility, equity, social justice, community, and diversity.

e) Lead with interpersonal and communication skill, social-emotional insight, and understanding of all students' and staff members' backgrounds and cultures.

f) Provide moral direction for the school and promote ethical and professional behavior among faculty and staff.

Standard Three: Equity and Cultural Responsiveness

Effective educational leaders strive for equity of educational opportunity and culturally responsive practices to promote each student's academic success and well-being. Effective Leaders:

a) Ensure that each student is treated fairly, respectfully, and with an understanding of each student's culture and context.

b) Recognize, respect, and employ each student's strengths, diversity, and culture as assets for teaching and learning.

c) Ensure that each student has equitable access to effective teachers, learning opportunities, academic and social support, and other resources necessary for success.

d) Develop student policies and address student misconduct in a positive, fair, and unbiased manner.

e) Confront and alter institutional biases of student marginalization, deficit-based schooling, and low expectations associated with race, class, culture and language, gender and sexual orientation, and disability or special status.

f) Promote the preparation of students to live productively in and contribute to the diverse cultural contexts of a global society.

g) Act with cultural competence and responsiveness in their interactions, decision-making, and practice.

h) Address matters of equity and cultural responsiveness in all aspects of leadership.

Standard Four: Curriculum, Instruction, and Assessment

Effective educational leaders develop and support intellectually rigorous and coherent systems of curriculum, instruction, and assessment to promote each student's academic success and well-being. Effective Leaders:

a) Implement coherent systems of curriculum, instruction, and assessment that promote the mission, vision, and core values of the school, embody high expectations for student learning, align with academic standards, and are culturally responsive.

b) Align and focus systems of curriculum, instruction, and assessment within and across grade levels to promote student academic success, love of learning, the identities and habits of learners, and healthy sense of self.

c) Promote instructional practice that is consistent with knowledge of child learning and development, effective pedagogy, and the needs of each student.

d) Ensure instructional practice that is intellectually challenging, authentic to student experiences, recognizes student strengths, and is differentiated and personalized.

e) Promote the effective use of technology in the service of teaching and learning.

f) Employ valid assessments that are consistent with knowledge of child learning and development and technical standards of measurement.

g) Use assessment data appropriately and within technical limitations to monitor student progress and improve instruction.

Standard Five: Community of Care and Support for Students

Effective educational leaders cultivate an inclusive, caring, and supportive school community that promotes the academic success and well-being of each student. Effective Leaders:

a) Build and maintain a safe, caring, and healthy school environment that meets that the academic, social, emotional, and physical needs of each student.

b) Create and sustain a school environment in which each student is known, accepted and valued, trusted and respected, cared for, and encouraged to be an active and responsible member of the school community.

c) Provide coherent systems of academic and social supports, services, extracurricular activities, and accommodations to meet the range of learning needs of each student.

d) Promote adult–student, student–peer, and school–community relationships that value and support academic learning and positive social and emotional development.

e) Cultivate and reinforce student engagement in school and positive student conduct.

f) Infuse the school's learning environment with the cultures and languages of the school's community.

Standard Six: Professional Capacity of School Personnel

Effective educational leaders develop the professional capacity and practice of school personnel to promote each student's academic success and well-being. Effective Leaders:

a) Recruit, hire, support, develop, and retain effective and caring teachers and other professional staff and form them into an educationally effective faculty.

b) Plan for and manage staff turnover and succession, providing opportunities for effective induction and mentoring of new personnel.

c) Develop teachers' and staff members' professional knowledge, skills, and practice through differentiated opportunities for learning and growth, guided by understanding of professional and adult learning and development.

d) Foster continuous improvement of individual and collective instructional capacity to achieve outcomes envisioned for each student.

e) Deliver actionable feedback about instruction and other professional practice through valid, research-anchored systems of supervision and evaluation to support the development of teachers' and staff members' knowledge, skills, and practice.

f) Empower and motivate teachers and staff to the highest levels of professional practice and to continuous learning and improvement.

g) Develop the capacity, opportunities, and support for teacher leadership and leadership from other members of the school community.

h) Promote the personal and professional health, well-being, and work–life balance of faculty and staff.

i) Tend to their own learning and effectiveness through reflection, study, and improvement, maintaining a healthy work–life balance.

Standard Seven: Professional Community for Teachers and Staff

Effective educational leaders foster a professional community of teachers and other professional staff to promote each student's academic success and well-being. Effective Leaders:

a) Develop workplace conditions for teachers and other professional staff that promote effective professional development, practice, and student learning.

b) Empower and entrust teachers and staff with collective responsibility for meeting the academic, social, emotional, and physical needs of each student, pursuant to the mission, vision, and core values of the school.

c) Establish and sustain a professional culture of engagement and commitment to shared vision, goals, and objectives pertaining to the education of the whole child; high expectations for professional work; ethical and equitable practice; trust and open communication; and collaboration, collective efficacy, and continuous individual and organizational learning and improvement.

d) Promote mutual accountability among teachers and other professional staff for each student's success and the effectiveness of the school as a whole.

e) Develop and support open, productive, caring, and trusting working relationships among leaders, faculty, and staff to promote professional capacity and the improvement of practice.

f) Design and implement job-embedded and other opportunities for professional learning collaboratively with faculty and staff.

g) Provide opportunities for collaborative examination of practice, collegial feedback, and collective learning.

h) Encourage faculty-initiated improvement of programs and practices.

Standard Eight: Meaningful Engagement of Families and Community

Effective educational leaders engage families and the community in meaningful, reciprocal, and mutually beneficial ways to promote each student's academic success and well-being. Effective Leaders:

a) Are approachable, accessible, and welcoming to families and members of the community.

b) Create and sustain positive, collaborative, and productive relationships with families and the community for the benefit of students.

c) Engage in regular and open two-way communication with families and the community about the school, students, needs, problems, and accomplishments.

d) Maintain a presence in the community to understand its strengths and needs, develop productive relationships, and engage its resources for the school.

e) Create means for the school community to partner with families to support student learning in and out of school.

f) Understand, value, and employ the community's cultural, social, intellectual, and political resources to promote student learning and school improvement.

g) Develop and provide the school as a resource for families and the community.

h) Advocate for the school and district and for the importance of education and student needs and priorities to families and the community.

i) Advocate publicly for the needs and priorities of students, families, and the community.

j) Build and sustain productive partnerships with public and private sectors to promote school improvement and student learning.

Standard Nine: Operations and Management

Effective educational leaders manage school operations and resources to promote each student's academic success and well-being. Effective Leaders:

a) Institute, manage, and monitor operations and administrative systems that promote the mission and vision of the school.

b) Strategically manage staff resources, assigning and scheduling teachers and staff to roles and responsibilities that optimize their professional capacity to address each student's learning needs.

c) Seek, acquire, and manage fiscal, physical, and other resources to support curriculum, instruction, and assessment; student learning community; professional capacity and community; and family and community engagement.

d) Are responsible, ethical, and accountable stewards of the school's monetary and nonmonetary resources, engaging in effective budgeting and accounting practices.

e) Protect teachers' and other staff members' work and learning from disruption.

f) Employ technology to improve the quality and efficiency of operations and management.

g) Develop and maintain data and communication systems to deliver actionable information for classroom and school improvement.

h) Know, comply with, and help the school community understand local, state, and federal laws, rights, policies, and regulations so as to promote student success.

i) Develop and manage relationships with feeder and connecting schools for enrollment management and curricular and instructional articulation.

j) Develop and manage productive relationships with the central office and school board.

k) Develop and administer systems for fair and equitable management of conflict among students, faculty and staff, leaders, families, and community.

l) Manage governance processes and internal and external politics toward achieving the school's mission and vision.

Standard Ten: School Improvement

Effective educational leaders act as agents of continuous improvement to promote each student's academic success and well-being. Effective Leaders:

a) Seek to make school more effective for each student, teachers and staff, families, and the community.

b) Use methods of continuous improvement to achieve the vision, fulfill the mission, and promote the core values of the school.

c) Prepare the school and the community for improvement, promoting readiness, an imperative for improvement, instilling mutual commitment and accountability, and developing the knowledge, skills, and motivation to succeed in improvement.

d) Engage others in an ongoing process of evidence-based inquiry, learning, strategic goal setting, planning, implementation, and evaluation for continuous school and classroom improvement.

e) Employ situationally appropriate strategies for improvement, including transformational and incremental, adaptive approaches and attention to different phases of implementation.

f) Assess and develop the capacity of staff to assess the value and applicability of emerging educational trends and the findings of research for the school and its improvement.

g) Develop technically appropriate systems of data collection, management, analysis, and use, connecting as needed to the district office and external partners for support in planning, implementation, monitoring, feedback, and evaluation.

h) Adopt a systems perspective and promote coherence among improvement efforts and all aspects of school organization, programs, and services.

i) Manage uncertainty, risk, competing initiatives, and politics of change with courage and perseverance, providing support and encouragement, and openly communicating the need for, process for, and outcomes of improvement efforts.

j) Develop and promote leadership among teachers and staff for inquiry, experimentation and innovation, and initiating and implementing improvement.

Appendix D

National Association of Secondary School Principals 21st-Century Skills

Educational Leadership

Setting Instructional Direction

- ◆ Implementing strategies for improving teaching and learning including putting programs and improvement efforts into action;
- ◆ Developing a vision and establishing clear goals;
- ◆ Providing direction in achieving stated goals;
- ◆ Encouraging others to contribute to goal achievement;
- ◆ Securing commitment to a course of action from individuals and groups.

Teamwork

- ◆ Seeking and encouraging involvement of team members;
- ◆ Modeling and encouraging the behaviors that move the group to task completion;
- ◆ Supporting group accomplishment.

Sensitivity

- ◆ Perceiving the needs and concerns of others;
- ◆ Dealing tactfully with others in emotionally stressful situations or in conflict;
- ◆ Knowing what information to communicate and to whom;
- ◆ Relating to people of varying ethnic, cultural, and religious backgrounds.

Resolving Complex Problems

Judgment

- ◆ Reaching logical conclusions and making high-quality decisions based on available information;
- ◆ Giving priority and caution to significant issues;
- ◆ Seeking out relevant data, facts, and impressions;
- ◆ Analyzing and interpreting complex information.

Results Orientation

- ◆ Assuming responsibility;
- ◆ Recognizing when a decision is required;
- ◆ Taking prompt action as issues emerge;

♦ Resolving short-term issues while balancing them against long-term objectives.

Organizational Ability

♦ Planning and scheduling one's own and the work of others so that resources are used appropriately;
♦ Scheduling flow of activities;
♦ Establishing procedures to monitor projects;
♦ Practicing time and task management;
♦ Knowing what to delegate and to whom.

Communication

Oral Communication

♦ Clearly communicating;
♦ Making oral presentations that are clear and easy to understand.

Written Communication

♦ Expressing ideas clearly in writing;
♦ Demonstrating technical proficiency;
♦ Writing appropriately for different audiences.

Developing Self and Others

Development of Others

♦ Teaching, coaching, and helping others;
♦ Providing specific feedback based on observations and data.

Understanding Own Strengths and Weaknesses

♦ Understanding personal strengths and weaknesses;
♦ Taking responsibility for improvement by actively pursuing developmental activities;
♦ Striving for continuous learning.

Source: *Selecting and Developing the 21st Century Principal Skills Assessment*, NASSP (2000).

National Association of Elementary School Principals Standards

Standard One: Balance Management and Leadership Roles

Effective principals lead schools in a way that places student and adult learning at the center.

Standard Two: Set High Expectations and Standards

Effective principals set high expectations and standards for the academic and social development of all students and the performance of adults.

Standard Three: Demand Content and Instruction That Ensures Student Achievement

Effective principals demand content and instruction that ensure student achievement of agreed-upon academic standards.

Standard Four: Create a Culture of Adult Learning

Effective principals create a culture of continuous learning for adults tied to student learning and other school goals.

Standard Five: Use Data as a Diagnostic Tool

Effective principals use multiple sources of data as diagnostic tools to assess, identify, and apply instructional improvement.

Standard Six: Actively Engage the Community

Effective principals actively engage the community to create shared responsibility for student and school success.

Source: *Leading Learning Communities: NAESP Standards for What Principals Should Know and Be Able to Do, 2nd edition.* (2008). NAESP: Alexandria, VA.

International Society for Technology in Education Standards for School Administrators

1. Visionary Leadership

Educational Administrators inspire and lead development and implementation of a shared vision for comprehensive integration of technology to promote excellence and support transformation throughout the organization. Educational Administrators:

a) Inspire and facilitate among all stakeholders a shared vision of purposeful change that maximizes use of digital-age resources to meet and exceed learning goals, support effective instructional practice, and maximize performance of district and school leaders.

b) Engage in an ongoing process to develop, implement, and communicate technology-infused strategic plans aligned with a shared vision.

c) Advocate on local, state, and national levels for policies, programs, and funding to support implementation of a technology-infused vision and strategic plan.

2. Digital-Age Learning Culture

Educational Administrators create, promote, and sustain a dynamic, digital-age learning culture that provides a rigorous, relevant, and engaging education for all students. Educational Administrators:

a) Ensure instructional innovation focused on continuous improvement of digital-age learning.

b) Model and promote the frequent and effective use of technology for learning.

c) Provide learner-centered environments equipped with technology and learning resources to meet the individual, diverse needs of all learners.

d) Ensure effective practice in the study of technology and its infusion across the curriculum.

e) Promote and participate in local, national, and global learning communities that stimulate innovation, creativity, and digital-age collaboration.

3. Excellence in Professional Practice

Educational Administrators promote an environment of professional learning and innovation that empowers educators to enhance student learning through the infusion of contemporary technologies and digital resources. Educational Administrators:

a) Allocate time, resources, and access to ensure ongoing professional growth in technology fluency and integration.

b) Facilitate and participate in learning communities that stimulate, nurture, and support administrators, faculty, and staff in the study and use of technology.

c) Promote and model effective communication and collaboration among stakeholders using digital-age tools.

d) Stay abreast of educational research and emerging trends regarding effective use of technology and encourage evaluation of new technologies for their potential to improve student learning.

4. Systemic Improvement

Educational Administrators provide digital-age leadership and management to continuously improve the organization through the effective use of information and technology resources. Educational Administrators:

a) Lead purposeful change to maximize the achievement of learning goals through the appropriate use of technology and media-rich resources.

b) Collaborate to establish metrics, collect and analyze data, interpret results, and share findings to improve staff performance and student learning.

c) Recruit and retain highly competent personnel who use technology creatively and proficiently to advance academic and operational goals.

d) Establish and leverage strategic partnerships to support systemic improvement.

e) Establish and maintain a robust infrastructure for technology including integrated, interoperable technology systems to support management, operations, teaching, and learning.

5. Digital Citizenship

Educational Administrators model and facilitate understanding of social, ethical, and legal issues and responsibilities related to an evolving digital culture. Educational Administrators:

a) Ensure equitable access to appropriate digital tools and resources to meet the needs of all learners.

b) Promote, model, and establish policies for safe, legal, and ethical use of digital information and technology.

c) Promote and model responsible social interactions related to the use of technology and information.

d) Model and facilitate the development of a shared cultural understanding and involvement in global issues through the use of contemporary communication and collaboration tools.

ISTE Standards for Administrators

ISTE Standards for Administrators, © 2009, ISTE® (International Society for Technology in Education), iste.org. All rights reserved.

■ Appendix G   Sample Case

The following relatively minor case is presented to show how the previous analysis questions can be used to find problems in leadership skill and make recommendations for professional development and school improvement.

"What Not to Wear"

Ted Smith was in his first year teaching 8th grade at Southwest Middle School. He had six years of previous teaching experience at another school with very good evaluations. He was popular with the students, but had little interaction with other teachers. He set high expectations and his students scored higher than the district average on various normed and criteria-referenced tests. He appeared to enjoy teaching at Southwest and never voiced complaints.

In January, four other 8th-grade teachers came to the principal's office with concerns about Mr. Smith's dress. The principal, Mrs. White, was surprised to see the teachers so upset and frustrated with the situation. They reported that they had observed Mr. Smith coming to school most days with jeans, T-shirts, and tennis shoes. They felt this was against policy that required "appropriate and professional dress." They wanted to know why the principal had allowed this to continue.

Mrs. White said that she knew Mr. Smith did not dress as nicely as most others, but that he had appeared to dress neatly and had never received any complaints before. The teachers remarked that they had heard complaints from many others and that his dress was unprofessional and embarrassing. They felt he was a poor model for the students and should not be given a new contract unless his dress met the policy. One of the teachers reminded the principal that she had made many comments about following policy during the year, but did not understand how Mr. Smith got away with not following policy. Mrs. White said she would meet with Mr. Smith at the end of the day to discuss the matter.

Before reviewing the analysis on the following pages, what would you do?

It should be noted that in giving this case to experienced administrators, many simply said to call in Mr. Smith and inform him that his dress must improve and meet written policy – case closed, on to the next one. Keep in mind that although this case appears to be more of a management issue than a leadership or instructional issue, if problems are found in decisions, communication, groups working together, culture, etc., these are all necessary skills for increasing learning and, therefore, must be addressed.

Consider whether the following analysis provides better information and leads to more appropriate actions than your initial reaction. The following analysis used the questions from each of skill areas provided in this section. Many of the areas of analysis overlap with others. For example, improper style, decision-making, or communication can cause conflict and/or decrease motivation – each area affects other areas. Thus, there is overlap in defining the problem and considering actions to take. The leader must summarize and prioritize data collected from the analysis and then plan appropriate action.

Trust

Aspects of the Problem Found

Little trust by the other teachers that the principal would take action
No evidence of trusting relationships among 8th-grade teachers

Actions to Be Taken

Follow through on the promise to meet with Mr. Smith and correct the problem
Ensure that all faculty understand the definition of professional dress and the role the principal will play if policy is not met
Set up meetings with the 8th-grade teachers for sharing of idea, concerns, and goals. Allow teachers the opportunity of better know one another

Vision

Aspects of the Problem Found

No clear, shared vision on how the staff should dress
No shared understanding of the definition of "appropriate and professional"
Currently no plans to address professional dress
A sense of distrust by some teachers whether the principal enforces policy uniformly

Actions to Be Taken

Choose a participatory or collaborative strategy to gather information for consensus on appropriate and professional dress
Include an interpretation of the definition of appropriate dress in the Teacher Handbook
Meet with or survey staff for other concerns in policy that the principal should address
Follow up with the teachers to develop a higher degree of trust

Decision-Making

Aspects of the Problem Found

No clear knowledge on the extent of the problem. Are other teachers concerned? Are there others besides Mr. Smith that are not meeting policy?

No information on how this affects learning

No generation of alternatives to deal with Mr. Smith

What decision model should be used?

How many should be involved?

Actions to Be Taken

Meet with members of diverse formal and informal groups to ascertain the extent and magnitude of the problem

Since staff has a high level of interest and expertise on dress and buy-in is needed, seek a consensus through collaboration

Since this affects all staff, include all staff in the collaboration

Provide adequate time for staff to reach consensus

Give students a voice in the effects on the culture of the school and their learning

Communication

Aspects of the Problem Found

The policy lacks needed detail and/or the leader has not clarified the policy

The concern has bothered staff for many months and was not voiced before – Why?

What other concerns are present and not reported to the principal?

Lack of agreement/understanding of the policy between the principal and staff

Actions to Be Taken

Ensure adequate detail is provided with the policy

Communicate both orally and in writing the expectations for staff dress

Take steps to inform staff of your desire and expectation to receive concerns

Provide various avenues for soliciting concerns, e.g., meet with departments on a regular basis, take time to visit with staff and students before and after school, and promote an open-door policy

Assess the level of communication between yourself and staff and seek a better network

Conflict

Aspects of the Problem Found

A misunderstanding of the role of the principal and teachers in addressing an issue policy

No clear expectation on how teachers should voice concerns

The teachers view the issue as embarrassing, not an opportunity for
improvement

No steps taken to resolve conflict between teachers

Actions to Be Taken

Clarify and communicate the role of the principal and teacher in issues
of policy

Elaborate to staff your desire to hear concerns and address concerns for
improvements to the school and each of its members

Provide staff development for conflict resolution at the personal and
department level

Gather as many alternatives as possible before making a decision

Model conflict resolution for staff

Motivation

Aspects of the Problem Found

The needs of the 8th-grade teachers are not being met

Mr. Smith's needs are not in line with the organizational needs

Mr. Smith does not appear to belong to any groups of faculty

Consider a mentor or buddy system for new teachers

Actions to Be Taken

Use the satisficing model and seek consensus to ensure needs are met
and aligned with the organizations needs and expectations

Plan for all staff to be part of formal or informal groups

Group Processes

Aspects of the Problem Found

Is Mr. Smith in an informal group? If not, why?

Does Mr. Smith participate in the formal 8th-grade group? If not, why?

Does the 8th-grade faculty have professionalism as one of its goals?

The 8th-grade teachers have not developed trust and openness to discuss concerns

How often does the 8th-grade faculty meet? Are their meetings run
effectively?

Have the 8th-grade teachers been trained in leading and being a member of a group?

Actions to Be Taken

Meet with Mr. Smith and discuss communication and collaboration with other 8th-grade teachers and staff

Provide training for the grade-level or department chair on leading meetings

Provide training for others to be effective group members and develop mutual trust

Leadership Style
Aspects of the Problem Found

Teachers are asking the principal to use a directive style with an experienced teacher

Actions to Be Taken

Begin with using a coaching or democratic leadership style with Mr. Smith and ascertain whether this is successful. If not, you may need to use directive until a more positive relationship is built.

Strive for additional referent (shared beliefs, values) power and/or expert power in communications, decisions, and group processes

Power
Aspects of the Problem Found

Teachers display a very little degree of power in resolving the issue with Mr. Smith

Actions to Be Taken

Meet with the 8th-grade teachers and reach consensus on expectations and the power to confront each other in grade-level meetings.

Culture/Climate
Aspects of the Problem Found

Lack of a culture of open communications

Lack a culture of professionalism in dress

At present, no time or resources given to this issue

Climate of frustration and ill feeling among some 8th-grade teachers

No assessments on climate are available or scheduled

Actions to Be Taken

Meet with faculty and communicate the desire and necessity for open communication.

Meet and find consensus on professional dress

Take extra time and effort in meeting the needs of the concerned 8th-grade teachers

Plan periodic assessments of school climate and take measures to address any concerns

Change

Aspects of the Problem Found

_____

_____

Actions to Be Taken

_____

_____

No major change efforts planned

Evaluation

Aspects of the Problem Found

Adequate information on dress is not part of hiring or induction practices
Periodic assessments of climate, concerns, and needs not used

Actions to Be Taken

Review hiring information and ensure issues of professional dress are included

Develop and use assessments at the beginning, middle, and end of the year to include measurements on climate, communication, and any others issues deemed important to staff and students

As a manger, one might simply decide to tell Mr. Smith to dress according to policy. As an instructional leader, however, one is very concerned with developing Mr. Smith since he appears to be an effective teacher. The leader would also be concerned with having the 8th-grade teachers work more effectively together – a skill needed to improve instruction and increase learning. The leader would also focus on increasing his/her skill in any of the other areas that surface as needing improvement. Keeping the focus on changes to increase learning, improve the overall school, and develop self and others is one difference between mangers and leaders. Your internship should focus on leading, not managing. Develop your skills and keep the proper focus.

Interns are expected to assess, monitor, and utilize ongoing reflection and evaluation of their skill development. Although skill development is essential for success in school leadership, reflection is also imperative for knowledge, disposition, and the ethical beliefs that guide actions. Skill without knowledge, appropriate disposition, or ethical belief will do little to develop others and meet the learning and developmental needs of the students.

References

Adams, G. B. (2011, Summer). The problem of administrative evil in a culture of technical rationality. *Public Integrity*, 13(3), 275–284.

Adams, G. B., & Balfour, D. L. (1998). *Unmasking administrative evil*. Thousand Oaks, CA: Sage.

Adams, G. B., & Balfour, D. L. (2009). Ethical failings, incompetence, and administrative evil: Lessons from Katrina and Iraq. In Raymond Cox (Ed.), *Ethics and Integrity in public administration: Concepts and cases* (pp. 40–61). Armonk, NY: M.E. Sharpe.

Anderson, G. (2009). *Advocacy leadership: Toward a post-reform agenda in education*. New York: Routledge.

Anyon, J. (2009). *Theory and educational research: Toward critical social explanation*. New York and London: Routledge.

Anyon, J. (2011, August 2). Review of advocacy leadership: Toward a post-reform agenda in education. Education Review by Gary L. Anderson. *Education Review*, 14. Retrieved from: http://www.edrev.info/reviews/rev1108.pdf

Baker, D. (2014). *The schooled society: The educational transformation of global culture*. Stanford, CA: Stanford University Press.

Barnard, C. I. (1938). *Functions of an executive*. Cambridge, MA: Harvard University Press.

Batagiannis, S. C. (2011). Promise and possibility for aspiring principals: An emerging leadership identity through learning to do action research. *The Qualitative Report*, 16(5), 1304–1329. Retrieved from http://nsuworks.nova.edu/tqr/vol16/iss5/6.

Bennis, W. (1989). *On becoming a leader*. Reading, MA: Addison Wesley.

Bennis, W. (2000). *Managing the dream*. Cambridge, MA: Perseus Publishing.

Bennis, W. (2003). *On becoming a leader* (Revised ed.). Cambridge, MA: Perseus Publishing.

Berliner, D. C. (2006). Our impoverished view of educational reform. *Teachers College Record*, 108(6), 949–995.

Berliner, D.C. (2009). *Poverty and potential: Out-of-school factors and school success*. Boulder and Tempe: Education and the Public Interest Center & Education Policy Research Unit. Retrieved from: http://epicpolicy.org/publication/poverty-and-potential

Berliner, D.C. & Glass, G.V. (2014). *50 myths & lies that threaten America's public schools: The real crisis in education.* New York: Teachers College Press.

Blackmore, J. (2009). Leadership for social justice: A transnational dialogue. *Journal of Research on Leadership Education,* 4, 1–10.

Branch, G. F., Hanushek, E. A., & Rivkin, S. G. (2013). School leaders matter: Measuring the impact of effective principals. *Education Next,* 13(1), 62–69.

Brody, J. L., Vissa, J., & Weathers, J. M. (2010). School leader professional socialization: The contribution of focused observation. *Journal of Research on Leadership Education,* 5(14), 611–651.

Brown, K. M. (2004). Leadership for social justice and equity: Weaving a transformative framework and pedagogy. *Educational Administration Quarterly,* 40, 79–110.

Brown, K. M. (2006). Leadership for social justice and equity: Evaluating a transformative framework and andragogy. *Educational Administration Quarterly,* 42, 700–745.

Browne-Ferrigno, T. (2003). Becoming a principal: Role conception, initial socialization, role-identity transformation, purposeful engagement. *Educational Administration Quarterly,* 39(4), 468–503.

Browne-Ferrigno, T. (2011). Mandated university-district partnerships for principal preparation: Professors' perspectives upon required program redesign. *Journal of School Leadership,* 21, 735–756.

Browne-Ferrigno, T., & Muth, R. (2006). Leadership mentoring and situated learning: Catalysts for principalship readiness and lifelong mentoring. *Mentoring & Tutoring: Partnership in Learning,* 14(3), 275–295.

Bryk, A. S., Sebring, P. B., Allensworth, E., Luppescu, S., & Easton, J. Q. (2010). *Organizing schools for improvement: Lessons from Chicago.* Chicago: University of Chicago Press.

Bustamante, R.M., Nelson, J.A., & Onwuegbuzie, A.J. (2009). Assessing schoolwide cultural competence: Implications for school leadership preparation. *Educational Administration Quarterly,* 45(5), 793–827.

Carnegie, D. (1993). *The leader in you.* New York: Simon & Schuster.

Charmaz, K. (2005). Grounded theory in the 21st century: Applications for advancing social justice studies. In N. K. Denzin & Y. S. Lincoln (Eds.), *The Sage handbook of qualitative research* (3rd ed., pp. 443–466). Thousand Oaks, CA: Sage.

Clark, R. E. (2012). *Learning from media: Arguments, analysis and evidence* (2nd ed.). Charlotte, NC: Information Age Publishing, Inc.

Cooperrider, D. L., & Srivasrtva, S. (1987). Appreciative inquiry in organizational life. In R. W. Woodman & W. A. Pasmore (Eds.), *Research in organizational change and development* (Vol. 1, pp. 129–169). Stamford, CT: JAI Press.

Cooperrider, D. L., & Whitney, D. (2005). A positive revolution in change: Appreciative inquiry. In D. L. Cooperrider, P. Sorenson, T. Yeager & D. Whitney (Eds.), *Appreciative inquiry: Foundations in positive organization development* (pp. 9–33). Champaign, IL: Stipes.

Council of Chief State School Officers (2008). *National policy standards: ISLLC 2008.* Washington, DC: Council of Chief State School Officers.

Covey, S. R. (1989). *The seven habits of highly effective people.* New York: Simon & Schuster.

Covey, S. R. (2009). *The speed of trust: Live from L.A.* New York: Covey.

Creasap, S. A., Peters, A. L., & Uline, C. L. (2005). The effects of guided reflection on educational leadership practice: Mentoring and portfolio writing as a means to transformative learning for early career principals. *Journal of School Leadership, 15*(4), 352–386.

Crow, G. M. (2012). A critical-constructivist perspective on mentoring and coaching for leadership. In S. J. Fletcher & C. A. Mullin (Eds.), *Sage handbook on mentoring and coaching in education* (pp. 228–242). Thousand Oaks, CA: Sage Publications.

Dana, N. F. (2009). *Leading with passion and knowledge: The principal as action research.* Thousand Oaks, CA: Corwin Press.

Dantley, M. E., & Tillman, L. C. (2010). Social justice and moral transformative leadership. In C. Marshall & M. Oliva (Eds.), *Leadership for social justice: Making revolutions in education* (2nd ed., pp. 54–85). Boston, MA: Allyn & Bacon.

Darling-Hammond, L. (2007). The flat earth and education: How America's commitment to equity will determine our future. *Educational Researcher, 36,* 318–334.

Darling-Hammond, L., LaPointe, M., Meyerson, D., Orr, M. T., & Cohen, C. (2007). *Preparing school leaders for a changing world: Lessons from exemplary leadership development programs.* Stanford, CA: Stanford University, Stanford Education Leadership Institute. Retrieved from: http://www.wallacefoundation.org/knowledge-center/school-leadership/key-research/Documents/Preparing-School-Leaders.pdf

Darling-Hammond, L., Meyerson, D., LaPointe, M.M., & Orr, M.T. (2010). *Preparing principals for a changing world.* San Francisco, CA: Jossey-Bass.

Davis, S., Darling-Hammond, L., LaPointe, M., & Meyerson, D. (2005). Review of research. School leadership study. Developing successful principals. Retrieved from Palo Alto, CA: SELI The Finance Project.

De Pree, M. (1989). *Leadership is an art.* New York: Dell.

De Pree, M. (1993). *Leadership jazz.* New York: Dell.

Deschenes, S., Cuban, L., & Tyack, D. (2001). Mismatch: Historical perspectives on schools and students who don't fit them. *Teachers College Record, 103*(4), 525–547.

Dewey, J. (1933). *How we think.* Buffalo, NY: Prometheus Books.

Dickmann, M. H., & Stanford-Blair, N. (2002). *Connecting leadership to the brain*. Thousand Oaks, CA: Corwin Press.

Evans, R. (1996). *The human side of school change*. San Francisco: Jossey-Bass.

Fensterwald, J. (2015, May 15). Students get piece of the action after seeking a say in budget. *EdSource: Highlighting strategies for student success*. Retrieved from: http://edsource.org/2015/students-get-piece-of-the-action-after-seeking-a-say-in-budget/79194#.VWTkpc9VhBc

Frels, R. K., Newman, I., & Newman, C. (2015). Mentoring the next generation of mixed and multiple method researchers. In S. Hesse-Biber & R. Burke Johnson (Eds.), *Oxford handbook for mixed and multiple method research* (pp. 333–353). New York, NY: Oxford University Press.

French, J. R., & Raven, B. (1959). The bases for social power. In D. Cartwright (Ed.), *Studies of social power* (pp. 259–269). Ann Arbor: University of Michigan Press.

Fullan, M. (2001a). *Leading in a culture of change*. New York: John Wiley & Sons.

Fullan, M. (2001b). *The new meaning of educational change* (3rd ed.). New York: Teachers College Press.

Fullan, M. (2002). *Leading in a culture of change*. New York: John Wiley & Sons.

Gardner, J. D. (1990). *On leadership*. New York: The Free Press.

Gerstl-Pepin, C., Killeen, K., & Hasazi, S. (2006). Utilizing an "ethic of care" in leadership preparation. *Journal of Educational Administration, 44*(3), 250. Retrieved from: http://proquest.umi.com/pqdweb?did=1127945551&Fmt=7&clientId=15403&RQT=309&VName=PQD

Gerzon, M. (2006). *Leading through conflict*. Boston, MA: Harvard Business School Press.

Gestalt Shift. (1998). *Wittgenstein's logic of language, supplement to projects in philosophy*. Retrieved from: http://www.roangelo.net/logwitt/gestalt-shift.html. Accessed on 02/01/2016.

Getzels, J. W. (1958). Administration as a social process. In A. Halpin (Ed.), *Administration theory in education*. Chicago: University of Chicago Midwest Administration Center.

Glanz, J. (2014). *Action research: An educational leader's guide to school improvement* (3rd ed.). Lanham, MA: Rowman & Littlefield.

Glass, G. V. (2008). *Fertilizers, pills, and magnetic strips: The fate of public education in America*. Charlotte, NC: Information Age Publishing.

Goleman, D. (1998). *Working with emotional intelligence*. New York: Bantam Books.

Goleman, D. (2000, March–April). Leadership that gets results. *Harvard Business Review, 78*(2), 78–90.

Gorton, R. A., & Snowden, P. E. (2002). *School leadership and administration* (6th ed.). New York: McGraw-Hill.

Grant, C. A. & Sleeter, C. E. (1986). Race, class, and gender in education research: An argument for integrative analysis. *Review of Educational Research*, 56(2), 195–211.

Gray, C. (2007). *Good principals aren't born – They're mentored: Are we investing enough to get the school leaders we need?* Atlanta, GA: Southern Regional Education Board. Retrieved from: http://www. wallacefoundation.org/knowledge-center/school-leadership/ principal-training/Documents/Good-Principals-Arent-Born-Theyre-Mentored.pdf

Green, A. (2011). *Beyond wealth.* Hoboken, NJ: John Wiley & Sons, Inc.

Greenberg, J., & Baron, R. A. (1997). *Behavior in organizations* (6th ed.). Englewood Cliffs, NJ: Prentice Hall.

Hackett, P. T., & Hortman, J. W. (2008). The relationship of emotional competencies to transformational leadership: Using a corporate model to assess the dispositions of educational leaders. *Journal of Educational Research & Policy Studies*, 8(1), 92–111.

Hall, G. E., & Hord, S. M. (2001), *Implementing change: Patterns, principles, and potholes.* Boston, MA: Allyn and Bacon.

Hendricks, G., & Ludeman, K. (1996). *The corporate mystic: A guidebook for visionaries with their feet on the ground.* New York: Bantam Books.

Holter, A. C., Frabutt, J. M., & Nuzzi, R. J. (2014). Leading the way: Catholic school leaders and action research. *eJournal of Catholic Education in Australasia*, 1(1), 1–24.

Hoy, W. K., & Miskel, C. G. (2001). *Educational administration: Theory, research, and practice* (6th ed.). New York: McGraw-Hill.

Johnson, L., Adams Becker, S., Estrada, V., & Freeman, A. (2015). *NMC horizon report: 2015* (K-12 ed.). Austin, TX: The New Media Consortium.

Johnson, L., Smith, R., Willis, H., Levine, A., & Haywood, K. (2011). *The 2011 horizon report.* Austin, TX: The New Media Consortium.

Katz, M., & Rose, M. (Eds.). (2013). *Public education under siege.* Philadelphia, PA: University of Pennsylvania Press.

Kohn, A. (1993). *Punished by rewards.* Boston, MA: Houghton Mifflin.

Kolb, D. A. (1984). *Experiential learning: Experience as the source of learning and development.* Upper Saddle River, NJ: Prentice-Hall.

Kolb, D. A., Boyatzis, R. E., & Mainemelis, C. (2001). Experiential learning theory: Previous research and new directions. In R. J. Sternberg & L. F. Zhang (Eds.), *Perspectives on thinking, learning, and cognitive styles* (pp. 227–248). Mahwah, NJ: Lawrence Erlbaum Associates.

Koshy, V. (2005). *Action research for improving practice: A practical guide.* London: Paul Chapman Publishing.

Kotter, J. P. (1998). *What leaders really do* (Harvard Business Review on Leadership). Boston, MA: Harvard Business School Press.

Lave, L., & Wenger, E. (1991). *Situated learning: Legitimate peripheral participation*. Cambridge: Cambridge University Press.

Leithwood, K., Louis, K. S., Anderson, S., & Wahlstrom, K. (2004). *How leadership influences student learning*. New York: Wallace Foundation. http://mt.educarchile.cl/MT/jjbrunner/archives/libros/Leadership.pdf

Lemke, C., & Coughlin, E. (2009). The change agents. *Educational Leadership*, 67(1), 54–59.

Logan, J. P. (2014). *School leadership through action research*. Boston, MA: Pearson.

Louis, K. S., Leithwood, K., Wahlstrom, K. L., & Anderson, S. E. (2010). *Investigating the links to improved student learning: Final report of research findings*. Minneapolis, MN: University of Minnesota. Retrieved from: http://www.wallacefoundation.org/knowledge-center/school-leadership/key-research/Documents/Investigating-the-Links-to-Improved-Student-Learning.pdf

Marshall, C. (1988). Analyzing the culture of school leadership. *Education and Urban Society*, 20, 262–272.

Marshall, C., & Oliva, M. (Eds.). (2010). *Leadership for social justice: Making revolutions in education* (2nd ed.). Boston, MA: Allyn & Bacon.

Mast, J., Scribner, J., & Sanzo, K. (2011). Authentic planning for leadership preparation and development. *Educational Planning*, 20(2), 31–42.

McDonald, J., Mohr, N., & Dichter, A. (2007). *The power of protocols: An educator's guide to better practice* (2nd ed.) New York, NY: Teachers College Press.

McKenzie, K. B., Skrla, L., & Scheurich, J. J. (2006). Preparing instructional leadership for social justice. *Journal of School Leadership*, 16, 158–170.

Mills, G. E. (2014). *Action research: A guide for the teacher researcher* (5th ed.). Thousand Oaks, CA: Pearson.

Moses, M. (2002). *Embracing Race: Why we need race-conscious education policy*. New York, NY: Teachers College Press.

Murphy, J. (2002). Reculturing the profession of educational leadership: New blueprints. *Educational Administration Quarterly*, 38(2), 176–191.

Murphy, J., Shipman, N., & Pearlman, M. (1997, September). Strengthening educational leadership: The ISLLC standards, streamlined seminar, *NAESP*, 16(1), 1–4.

National Association of Elementary School Principals. (2008). *Leading learning communities* (2nd Ed.). Alexandria, VA: Author.

National Association of Secondary School Principals. (2000). *Selecting and Developing the 21st Century Principal Skills Assessment*. Reston, VA: National Association of Secondary School Principals.

National Association of Secondary School Principals. (2011). *Breaking ranks: A comprehensive framework for school improvement*. Reston, VA: Author.

National Council for Professors of Educational Administration. (2000, August). *Panel discussion with Joe Schneider, Neil Shipman, John Hoyle, and Chuck Achilles*. NCPEA Conference, Ypsilanti, MI.

National Policy Board for Educational Administration. (2015). *Professional Standards for Educational Leaders 2015*. Reston, VA: National Policy Board for Educational Administration.

Orr, M. T. (2006). Mapping innovation in leadership preparation in our nation's schools of education. *Phi Delta Kappan*, 87(7), 492–499.

Osterman, K., Furman, G., & Sernak, K. (2014). Action research in Ed.D. programs in educational leadership. *Journal of Research on Leadership Education*, 9(1), 85–105. doi:10.1177/1942775113498378

Osterman, K. F., & Kottkamp, R. B. (2004). *Reflective practice for educators* (2nd ed.) Thousand Oaks, CA: Corwin Press.

Perkins IV (Carl D. Perkins Career and Technical Education Improvement Act of 2006). Retrieved from: https://www.gpo.gov/fdsys/pkg/BILLS-109s250enr/pdf/BILLS-109s250enr.pdf

Prensky, M. (2001, October). Digital natives, digital immigrants. *On the Horizon*, Bradford, West Yorkshire, England: MCB University Press, 9(5), 1–6.

Rodgers, C. (2002). Defining reflection: Another look at John Dewey and reflective thinking. *Teachers College Record*, 14(4), 842–866.

Rucinski, D. A., & Bauch, P. A. (2006). Reflective, ethical, and moral constructs in educational leadership preparation: Effects on graduates' practices. *Journal of Educational Administration*, 44(5), 487. Retrieved from: http://proquest.umi.com/pqdweb?did=1105625181&Fmt=7&clientId=15403&RQT=309&VName=PQD

Russell, T., & Munby, H. (1991). Reframing: The role of experience in developing teachers' professional knowledge. In D. Schön (Ed.), *The reflective turn: Case studies in and on educational practice* (pp. 164–187). New York: Teachers College Press.

Sagor, R. (2009). Collaborative action research and school improvement: We can't have one without the other. *Journal of Curriculum and Instruction*, 3(19), 7–14. doi:10.3776/joci.2009.v3n1p7-14

Sanzo, K. (2016). *Strategies for developing and supporting school leaders: Stepping stones to great leadership*. New York: Routledge.

Sappington, N., Baker, P. J. Gardner, D., & Pacha, J. (2010). A signature pedagogy for leadership education: Preparing principals through participatory action research. *Planning and Changing*, 41(3/4), 249–273.

Schein, E. H. (1992). *Organizational culture and leadership*. San Francisco: Jossey-Bass.

Schön, D. A. (1987). *Educating the reflective practitioner*. San Francisco: Jossey-Bass.

Schön, D. (Ed.). (1991). *The reflective turn: Case studies in and on educational practice.* New York: Teachers College Press.

Senge, P. (1990, Fall). The leader's new work: Building learning organizations. *Sloan Management Review,* 32(1), 7–23.

Senge, P.M. (2009). The necessary revolution. *Leader to Leader,* 51(Winter), pp. 24–28.

Senge, P., Kleiner, A., Roberts, C., Ross, R., Roth, G., & Smith, B. (1996). *The dance of change: The challenges of sustaining momentum in learning organizations.* New York: Currency Doubleday.

Shoho, A., Barnett, B. G., & Martinez, P. (2012). Enhancing "OJT" internships with interactive coaching. *Planning & Changing,* 43(1–2), 161–182.

Simon, H.A. (1947). *Administrative Behavior.* New York: Macmillan.

Singleton, G.E., & Linton, C.W. (2005). *Courageous conversations about race: A field guide for achieving equity in schools.* Thousand Oaks, CA: Corwin Press.

Skrla, L., McKenzie, K., & Scheurich, J. (2008). *Equity audits: Leadership tools for developing equitable and excellent schools.* Thousand Oaks, CA: Corwin Press.

Solomon, G., & Schrum, L. (2010). *Web 2.0: New tools, new schools.* Eugene, OR: International Society for Technology in Education.

Svara, J. (2014). *The ethics primer for public administrators in government and nonprofit organizations* (2nd ed.). Burlington, MA: Jones & Bartlett Learning.

Taggart, G.L. & Wilson, A.P. (2005). *Promoting reflective thinking in teachers: 50 action strategies* (2nd ed.). Thousand Oaks, CA: Corwin Press.

Taylor, S., Rudolf, J., & Goldy, E. (2008). Teaching reflective practice in action science/action inquiry tradition: Key stages, concepts and practices. In P. Reason & H. Bradbury (Eds.), *The Sage handbook of action research: Participative inquiry and practice* (2nd ed., pp. 656–669). Los Angeles: Sage Publications.

Terry, K. (2010). *Building educational leadership capacity through a graduate action research course.* Retrieved from: http://files.eric.ed.gov/fulltext/ED509986.pdf

Terry, R. (1993). *Authentic leadership.* San Francisco, CA: Jossey-Bass.

Theoharis, G. (2007). Social justice educational leaders and resistance: Toward a theory of social justice leadership. *Educational Administration Quarterly,* 43(2), 221–258.

Thomas, K. (1976). Conflict and conflict management. In M. D. Dunnette (Ed.), *Handbook of industrial and organizational psychology* (pp. 889–936). Chicago: Rand McNally.

Tishman, S., Jay, E., & Perkins, D. M. (1993). Teaching thinking dispositions: From transmission to enculturation. *Theory into Practice,* 32, 147–153.

Tschannen-Moran, M. (2003). Transformational leadership and trust. In W.K. Hoy & C.G. Miskel (Eds.), *Studies in leading and organizing schools* (pp. 157–179). Charlotte, NC: Information Age Publishing.

Tyack, D. B. (1976). Ways of seeing: An essay on the history of compulsory schooling. *Harvard Educational Review*, 46(3), 355–389.

Tyack, D. B. (1993). Constructing difference: Historical reflections on school and social diversity. *Teachers College Record*, 95(1), 8–34.

Vickers, G. (1995). *The art of judgment: A study of policy making*. Thousand Oaks, CA: Sage.

Vygotsky, L. S. (1978). *Mind in society: The development of higher psychological processes*. Cambridge, MA: Harvard University Press.

Wagner, T. (1994). *How schools change: Lessons from three communities*. Boston, MA: Beacon Press.

Wagner, T., Kegan, R., Lahey, L., Lemons, R. W., Garnier, J., Helsing, R., & Rasussen, H. T. (2006). *Change leadership: A practical guide for transforming our schools*. San Francisco, CA: Jossey-Bass.

Weis, L. (1988). *Class, race, and gender in American education*. Albany, NY: SUNY Press.

Williams, E. J., Matthews, J., & Baugh, S. (2004). Developing a mentoring internship model for school leadership: Using legitimate peripheral participation. *Mentoring & Tutoring: Partnership in Learning*, 12(1), 53–70.

Wood, L., & Govender, B. (2013). "You learn from going through the process": The perceptions of South African school leaders about action research. *Action Research,* 11(2), 176–193.

Wright, R. J. (2014). *Research methods for counseling: An introduction*. Thousand Oaks, CA: Sage.

■ Index

accommodating in conflict resolution 133
action research process 88–9, 93–4, 151
Adams, G. B. 81
Adams Becker, S. 97
administrative manager 128
adult learning 57
affiliations/resources 79
affiliative leadership style 137–8
after-school mentoring/enrichment programs 103–4
Allensworth, E. 94
American Association of Colleges for Teacher Education (AACTE) 10
American Association of School Administrators (AASA) 10
Americans with Disabilities Act (ADA) 52
Anderson, G. 82, 83, 85
Anderson, S. 1, 94
Anyon, J. 82, 83
assessment and feedback 6–7
Association of School Business Officials (ASBO) 75
avoiding in conflict resolution 133

Baker, D. 82
Baker, P. J. 89
Balfour, D. L. 81
Barnard, C. I. 81
Baron, R. A. 140
Batagiannis, S. C. 91, 93
Bauch, P. A. 94
Baugh, S. 9
behavioral thinking in public schools 134
Bennis, W. 1, 85, 135
Berliner, D. C. 82
Blackmore, J. 81
Boyatzis, R. E. 89
Branch, G. F. 88
bring their own technology (BYOT) 45
Brody, J. L. 9
Brown, K. M. 81, 94, 95
Browne-Ferrigno, T. 9, 10, 89
Bryk, A. S. 94
budget supervision 75
business shadowing 104
Bustamante, R. M. 38
buy-in support in decision-making process 130

career fairs 104
Carnegie, D. 132
case-based teaching methods 89
change process 77, 186

Charmaz, K. 92
Children's Online Privacy Protection Act (COPA) 45
Clark, R. E. 99
cloud-based resources 97, 98
coaching leadership style 137
coercive power 138
Cohen, C. 88
collaborating in conflict resolution 133
collaborative leadership style 137
communication: in action research process 94; of meetings 136; overview 176; with partnerships 103; sample case 183; skills 131–3
community of care/support for students 170
community of learners 106
community/public relations 65
community reads programs 104
community resources 67
competence and observation 150
competencies in practice 126–7
competing in conflict resolution 133
compromising in conflict resolution 133
conference groups 109
conflict resolution 133–4, 184
conflicts of interest 119
Cooperrider, D. L. 85
Coughlin, E. 97
Council for the Accreditation of Educator Preparation (CAEP) 10
Council of Chief State School Officers (CCSSO) 10
Covey, S. R. 127, 131
Creasap, S. A. 94
critical lens in research 92
critical reasoning 151
Crow, G. M. 10
Cuban, L. 82
cultural diversity climate 36–7, 185–6

daily journal format 145
Dana, N. F. 93, 94
Dantley, M. E. 81
Darling-Hammond, L. 10, 81, 88, 89
Davis, S. 89
decision-making process 114–16, 129–31, 183
democracy 89, 137
De Pree, M. 85
Deschenes, S. 82
design/management in communication 132
development of self/others 176
Dewey, J. 105
Dichter, A. 109

Dickmann, M. H. 144
digital citizenship 179–80
digital resources for teaching/learning 97–8, 178
directive leadership style 137
disciplinary decisions 119
dispositions 14–16, 17, 94–6, 150
distributed leadership 63
district/school assessment 16–17
distrust concerns 127–8
dual college credit 104
Dweck, C. 55

Easton, J. 94
educational camps 104
Educational Leadership Constituent Council
    (ELCC) 11
ELCC/NELP standards 4
equity and cultural responsiveness 38, 169–70
essential competencies 144, 151
Estrada, V. 97
ethical and critical reasoning: avoiding ethical
    traps 118–21; decision-making process 114–16;
    leadership focus 111–12; overview 151; power of
    vision 110–11; preservation of 116–18; principal
    and 121–2; professional norms 168–9; standards
    29; teacher/principal evaluations 113–14; use of
    power 138–9
evaluation component: monitoring of 146–7; with
    partnerships 103; sample case 186; of student/
    personnel/program 143–4
Evans, R. 142
Every Student Succeeds Act (ESSA) 24
expert power 139

facility maintenance/safety/security 72
faculty/staff evaluation 59
Family Educational Rights and Privacy Act of 1974
    (FERPA) 70
Fensterwald, J. 87
food services 74
Frabutt, J. M. 89
Freeman, A. 97
Frels, R. K. 90
French, J. R. 138
Fullan, M. 126, 140–1, 142
Furman, G. 89

Gardner, D. 89
Gardner, J. D. 128
General Educational Development (GED) Test
    Coordination 104
general office/administrative technology 69–70
Gerstl-Pepin, C. 94
Gerzon, M. 81, 85
Glanz, J. 91
Glass, G. V. 82
Goldy, E. 107
Goleman, D. 94, 137
Gorton, R. A. 131
Govender, B. 91
Grant, C. A. 81

Gray, C. 88, 89, 90
Green, A. 127
Greenberg, J. 140
group processes 184–5

Hackett, P. T. 94
Hall, G. E. 142
Hanushek, E. A. 88
Hasazi, S. 94
Haywood, K. 91
hiring decisions 119
Holter, A. C. 89
Hord, S. M. 142
Horizon Report 98
Horton, J. W. 94
Hoy, W. K. 126, 129, 133

independent leading level in leadership development
    10
Individuals with Disabilities Education Improvement
    Act (IDEIA) 51
information giving/receiving 131–2
initial leading level in leadership development 10
instructional direction 175
intermittent journal format 145
International Center for Leadership in Education
    (ICLE) 55
International Society for Technology in Education
    (ISTE) for Administrators 100, 178–80
International Society for Technology in Education
    (ISTE) for Students 100
International Society for Technology in Education
    (ISTE) for Teachers 100
internship assessment: dispositions 14–16, 17;
    district/school assessment 16–17; other
    assessment/evaluations 16; overview 13;
    professional standards, self-assessment 13–14,
    17; summary 17; vita 13, 17
interns/internship: action research process 88–9,
    93–4, 151; dispositions/interpersonal skills 150;
    impact of 150; journals for reflection 108–9,
    144–6; logs and other tools 107–10, 146,
    149; outline of 7–8; portfolio organization/
    development 146, 152–3; roles and
    responsibilities 2–3; standards, leadership,
    activities 19–20; vita update 13, 17, 153; see also
    school leadership internship
interpersonal skills 94–6, 150
interviewing 125–6
issue/conflict resolution 61, 134

Jay, E. 94
Johnson, L. 91, 93, 97, 98
journals for reflection 108–9, 144–6

Kaiser Family Foundation 98
Katz, M. 82
Killeen, K. 94
knowledge in action research process 94
Kohn, A. 134–5
Kolb, D. A. 89, 95

Koshy, V. 91
Kotter, J. P. 128
Kottkamp, R. B. 94

Laissez-Faire leadership style 138
LaPointe, M. 88, 89
Lave, L. 9
leadership implementation: communication
    skills 131–3; competencies in practice 126–7;
    conflict resolution 133–4; developing trusting
    relationships 127–8; essential competencies
    144; experience 1; focus for success 111–12;
    initiating change 140–2; interviewing 125–6;
    journals for reflection 108–9, 144–6; managing
    group processes 135–7; motivating/developing
    others 134–5; networking 126; positive culture/
    climate of 139–40; preparation 89–90; realization
    of the vision 128–9; sample case 181–6; shared
    decisions 129–31; student/personnel/program
    evaluation 143–4; supporting others 137–8; using
    power ethically 138–9
learning-centered leaders 111–12
legitimate power 139
Leithwood, K. 1, 94
Lemke, C. 97, 98
lesbian, gay, bisexual, and transgender (LGBT)
    students 50
letter of application 153, 164–7
Levine, A. 91
Lewin, K. 126
Linton, C. W. 38
Local Control Funding Formula (LCFF) 87
local projects 123
logs and other tools 107–10, 146, 149
Louis, K. S. 1, 94
Ludeman, K. 142
Luppescu, S. 94

Mainemelis, C. 89
managing group processes 135–7
Marshall, C. 81
Mast, J. 102
Matthews, J. 9
McDonald, J. 109
McKenzie, K. 38, 94
meaningful engagement 172–3
meaning making and reflection 105–6
meeting rules 136
mentoring practices 5–6
Meyerson, D. 10, 88, 89
Mills, G. E. 92, 93
Miskel, C. G. 126, 129, 133
mission/vision 22, 169
mobile learning 97
Mohr, N. 109
monitoring/evaluating in communication 132
Moses, M. 81
motivating/developing others 134–5, 184
Munby, H. 106
Murphy, J. 11, 85
Muth, R. 10

National Association of Elementary School Principals
    (NAESP) 11, 40, 79, 177
National Association of Secondary School Principals
    (NASSP) 11, 175–6
National Board for Professional Teaching Standards
    (NBPTS) 11
National Council of Professors of Educational
    Administration (NCPEA) 11
National Policy Board for Educational
    Administration (NPBEA) 10, 13–14, 149, 168–74
Nelson, J. A. 38
networking 126
Newman, C. 90
Newman, I. 90
new technologies 152
Nuzzi, R. J. 89

observing level in leadership development 8–9
Oliva, M. 81
online learning communities 97
on-the-job experience 150
Onwuegbuzie, A. J. 38
operations and management 173–4
Orr, M. T. 88, 89
Osterman, K. F. 89, 93, 94

Pacha, J. 89
parent involvement 66
participative leadership style 9–10, 137
Pearlman, M. 11
Perkins, D. M. 94
personnel procedures 58, 143–4
Peters, A. L. 94
philosophical guiding questions 92
planning component with partnerships 102–3
portfolio organization/development 146, 152–3
positive culture/climate of leadership 139–40
power concept 138–9, 185
Prensky, M. 97
preservation of ethics 116–18
principal, ethical and critical reasoning 121–2
principal, evaluations 113–14
problem-based teaching methods 89
problem-solving 175–6
professional community 171–2
professional development plan 152
professional learning community (PLC) 62
professional standards 10–12, 13–14, 17, 149
Professional Standards for Educational Leaders
    (2015): achievement/testing and measurements
    46; affiliations/resources 79; budget supervision
    75; change process 77; co-curricular education
    supervision 48; collective decision-making 27;
    community/public relations 65; community
    resources 67; cultural diversity climate 36–7;
    curriculum analysis 40–1; data collection/
    analysis 24; distributed leadership 63; effective
    communication 25; equity in practice 38; ethics
    29; facility maintenance/safety/security 72;
    faculty/staff evaluation 59; food services 74;
    general office/administrative technology

69–70; history/traditions of school/community 33; instruction/instructional strategies 55–6; interpersonal relationships 32; introduction 1, 11–12; issue/conflict resolution 61; learning communities 62; learning/motivation theory 43; learning technology 44–5; local norms/ expectations 30; negotiating/consensus building 26; parent involvement 66; personnel procedures 58; philosophy of leadership 31; remediation strategies 53; school board policies/ procedures 34; school improvement planning 80; school operations/policies 71; school/ program scheduling 42; skill and performance activities 81–8, 86; social justice in 83–4; special populations 51–2; staff development/adult learning 57; standard one 21–7, 168; standard two 28–34, 168–9; standard three 169; standard four 39–46, 169–70; standard five 47–53, 170; standard six 54–9, 171; standard seven 60–3, 171–2; standard eight 64–7, 172–3; standard nine 68–75, 173–4; standard ten 76–80, 174; strategic planning 23; student discipline 49; student services 50; student transportation 73; teaching/ learning, current issues 78; vision/mission 22, 169
program evaluation 143–4
projects journal format 145
promotion decisions 119

quality concerns in decision-making process 130

Raven, B. 138
realization of the vision 128–9
reassignment decisions 119
referent power 139
reflection in action: defined 105–7; intern experience with 150–1; introduction 105; learning reflective practice 108; logs and other tools 107–10; reflection-on-action cycle 106–8
reflection-on-action cycle 106–8
remediation strategies 53
resistance to change 141–2
Response to Intervention (RtI) team 49
reward power 138
Rivkin, S. G. 88
Rodgers, C. 105, 106
roles and responsibilities 2–3
Rose, M. 82
Rucinski, D. A. 94
Rudolf, J. 107
rules for meetings 136
Russell, T. 106

Sagor, R. 93
Sanzo, K. 102
Sappington, N. 89, 91, 93
Schein, E. H. 139
Scheurich, J. J. 38, 94
Schön, D. 107, 108
school administrators and technology 99–100
school building internship supervisor 4–5
school improvement 80, 153, 174

School Improvement Plan (SIP) 80
school leadership internship: assessment and feedback 6–7; developmental nature of 8–10, 9; effective leadership preparation 89–90; ethical and critical reasoning 110–22; introduction 1; local projects 123; meeting professional standards 10–12; mentoring practices 5–6; overall plan report 124; quality experiences 89; reflection in action 105–10; roles and responsibilities 2–3; school building internship supervisor 4–5; school improvements 90–1; school partnerships 101–4; service activities 122–3; site supervisor, collaboration with 123; university advisor 3–4
school operations/policies 71
Schrum, L. 98
Scribner, J. 102
Sebring, P. B. 94
self-reflection process 92
Senge, P. 85, 142
sensitivity 175
Sernak, K. 89
service activities 122–3
shared decisions 129–31
Shipman, N. 11
Simon, H. A. 81
Singleton, G. E. 38
Site-Based Decision-Making (SBDM) team 63
site supervisor, collaboration with 123
Skrla, L. 38, 94
Sleeter, C. E. 81
Smith, R. 91
Snowden, P. E. 131
social hierarchies 92
social justice: action research process 88–9, 93–4; activities for 88; degrees of 152; disposition/ interpersonal skills 94–6; in internship 84–7, 86; opportunities for 87–8; overview 81–3; in professional standards 83–4; teaching methods and 89; technologies and 97–9
social policies/practices, consequences 92
Solomon, G. 98
special populations 51–2
Srivasrtva, S. 85
staff development 57
staff expertise in decision-making process 130
Stanford-Blair, N. 144
STEAM (science, technology, engineering, arts, and math) 97
STEM (science, technology, engineering, and math) 97
student evaluation 143–4
student transportation 73
summative reflection 109–10
Svara, J. 81
systemic improvement 179

Taggart, G. L. 144
Taylor, S. 107
teacher evaluations 113–14
teaching/learning, current issues 78
teamwork 175

technical assistance evaluation 104
technologies and social justice 97–9, 152
termination decisions 119
Terry, K. 81, 89
testing coordinators 104
Theoharis, G. 94
Thomas, K. 133
Tillman, L. C. 81
time factor in decision-making process 130
Tishman, S. 94
transmittal of feelings and impressions 131
trusting relationships 127–8, 182
Tschannen-Moran, M. 82
Tyack, D. 81, 82

Uline, C. L. 94
university advisor 3–4
University Council for Educational Administration
        (UCEA) 11

Vickers, G. 84–5
vision/mission 22, 169, 182
Vissa, J. 9
vita: FAQs 161–3; guidelines for development of
        158–61; overview 13, 17, 153; sample of 155–7
Vygotsky, L. S. 43

Wagner, T. 94, 142
Wahlstrom, K. 1, 94
Weathers, J. M. 9
weekly journal format 145
Weis, L. 81
Wenger, E. 9
Whitney, D. 85
Williams, E. J. 9
Willis, H. 91
Wilson, A. P. 144
Wood, L. 91
Wright, R. J. 90